Raising the Future

Navigating Parenting Styles for Modern Families

By
Well-Being Publishing

Copyright 2024 Well-Being Publishing. All rights reserved.

WELL-BEING PUBLISHING

No part of this book may be reproduced in any form or by any electronic or mechanical means including information storage and retrieval systems, without permission in writing from the author. The only exception is by a reviewer, who may quote short excerpts in a review.

Although the author and publisher have made every effort to ensure that the information in this book was correct at press time, the author and publisher do not assume and hereby disclaim any liability to any party for any loss, damage, or disruption caused by errors or omissions, whether such errors or omissions result from negligence, accident, or any other cause.

This publication is designed to provide accurate and authoritative information with regard to the subject matter covered. It is sold with the understanding that the publisher is not engaged in rendering professional services. If legal advice or other expert assistance is required, the services of a competent professional should be sought.

The fact that an organization or website is referred to in this work as a citation and/or a potential source of further information does not mean that the author or the publisher endorses the information the organization or website may provide or recommendations it may make.

Please remember that Internet websites listed in this work may have changed or disappeared between when this work was written and when it is read.

To you,
Thank you!

Table of Contents

Introduction: The Evolution of Parenting in the Modern World........ 1

Chapter 1: Understanding Parenting Styles.. 5
    The Four Classic Styles 5

Chapter 2: The Impact of Culture on Parenting.................................... 19
    Eastern vs. Western Approaches 19
    The Influence of Tradition and Modernity 23

Chapter 3: The Role of Gender in Parenting Practices........................ 27
    Challenging Gender Stereotypes.. 27
    Shaping Identity: Mothers and Fathers... 31

Chapter 4: Attachment Theory and Parenting...................................... 35
    Secure and Insecure Attachments 35
    Practical Strategies for Building Strong Bonds 38

Chapter 5: The Digital Age and Its Effect on Parental Guidance 42
    Navigating Screen Time 42
    Social Media: The Risks and Rewards 46

Chapter 6: Discipline and Setting Boundaries...................................... 49
    Effective Methods for Different Ages.. 49
    Balancing Leniency and Strictness 52

Chapter 7: Parenting and Emotional Intelligence 56
    Nurturing Empathy and Resilience.. 56
    Teaching Self-Regulation and Mindfulness 60

Chapter 8: Education and the Parental Role 64

The Home Learning Environment 64
Collaborating with Educators 67

Chapter 9: Support Systems and Their Importance in Parenting 71
Extended Family and Community Influence 71
The Value of Parenting Groups and Resources 74

Chapter 10: Addressing Special Needs and Inclusivity 78
Tailoring Your Approach 79
Advocacy and Accessibility 82

Chapter 11: Mental Health and Parenting 86
Recognizing Signs in Children 86
Prioritizing Self-Care for Parents and Caregivers 89

Chapter 12: Looking Ahead: Preparing Children for the Future 93
Fostering Independence and Responsibility 93
Encouraging a Growth Mindset 97
Online Review Request for This Book 100

Chapter 13: Embracing Your Unique Parenting Journey 101

Appendix A: Appendix 105
Resources for Further Reading 105
Support Networks and Professional Help 105
Checklists and Quick-Reference Guides 106
Resources for Further Reading 107
Support Networks and Professional Help 110
Checklists and Quick-Reference Guides 113

References 119

Introduction: The Evolution of Parenting in the Modern World

The landscape of parenting has undergone a seismic transformation over the past few decades. Once shaped by simple dictates of tradition and cultural norms, modern parenting now finds itself navigating a complex web of societal changes, technological advancements, and evolving family dynamics. This evolution has prompted many parents and caregivers to seek out new strategies and adapt their approaches to meet the diverse needs of their children.

It's no secret that parenting in the 21st century comes with its own set of unique challenges. From the pervasive influence of social media to the pressures of academic success, the environment in which we raise our children today is markedly different from that of any preceding generation. Yet, despite these changes, the core objective of parenting remains the same: to nurture and guide our children to become well-rounded, responsible, and emotionally healthy individuals.

As we delve into the intricacies of modern parenting, it's crucial to acknowledge that there is no one-size-fits-all approach. What works for one family may not be effective for another, and what resonates with one child may not resonate with their sibling. This realization underscores the importance of understanding different parenting styles and the impact they can have on a child's overall development.

Through the pages of this book, we'll explore various parenting styles, their characteristics, and their potential effects on children's growth and behavior. We'll delve into how culture, gender, and digitalization play pivotal roles in shaping parenting practices today. By examining these facets, our goal is to equip you with the knowledge and tools necessary to make informed decisions that align with your unique family dynamics.

Our journey begins with an overview of the four classic parenting styles: authoritative, authoritarian, permissive, and uninvolved. These styles serve as the foundational pillars upon which modern parenting has evolved. Each approach represents a distinct blend of parental responsiveness and demandingness, offering a framework within which parents can reflect on their own practices and aspirations. Understanding these styles will lay the groundwork for more nuanced discussions in the chapters to come.

One significant factor that shapes parenting styles is cultural background. The dichotomy between Eastern and Western parenting approaches provides a compelling testament to how deeply ingrained cultural values can influence our methods of raising children. While Western approaches might emphasize individuality and independence, Eastern methods often prioritize family cohesion and respect for authority. These cultural nuances offer invaluable insights into the diversity of parenting practices worldwide.

Gender roles, too, have traditionally played a significant role in how parenting responsibilities are divided. However, the modern world is increasingly challenging these stereotypes, encouraging a more equitable distribution of parenting duties. By recognizing and addressing the impact of gender on parenting, we can better understand the diverse roles that mothers and fathers can play in their children's lives, fostering more balanced and supportive environments.

As we move forward, attachment theory will provide us with essential insights into the importance of forming secure bonds with our children. The quality of these attachments can significantly influence a child's emotional and social development, laying the groundwork for healthy relationships in later life. We'll discuss practical strategies for building and maintaining these crucial bonds, ensuring that our children feel loved and supported at every stage of their development.

In today's digital age, the role of technology in parenting has become inevitable. From screen time management to navigating the world of social media, parents must equip themselves with the knowledge to guide their children through the digital landscape safely and responsibly. We'll examine the risks and rewards associated with these digital tools, helping you strike a balance that leverages technology's benefits while mitigating its downsides.

Balancing discipline and freedom is another cornerstone of effective parenting. This book will explore various methods of discipline, emphasizing techniques that are age-appropriate and sensitive to each child's unique temperament. Whether you're dealing with a toddler's tantrums or a teenager's rebellion, finding the right balance between leniency and strictness is key to fostering respect and trust within the family dynamic.

Emotional intelligence is also a critical component of child development. By nurturing empathy, resilience, and mindfulness, parents can equip their children with the tools they need to navigate life's challenges with confidence and grace. We'll discuss practical ways to cultivate these traits, contributing to the overall emotional well-being of your children.

The role of education extends beyond the classroom. Parents play a pivotal role in creating a conducive home learning environment and collaborating effectively with educators. We'll delve into strategies that support your child's academic journey, ensuring they receive the best possible guidance both at home and in school.

Parenting is not a solitary endeavor. The support systems we build around us—whether through extended family, community, or parenting groups—are invaluable resources that can offer insight, encouragement, and assistance. Drawing on these networks can provide much-needed support as you navigate the complexities of raising children.

As we address parenting special needs and inclusivity, it's critical to tailor your approach to meet the unique requirements of every child. Advocacy and accessibility form the bedrock of inclusive parenting, emphasizing that every child deserves the opportunity to thrive, regardless of their abilities or challenges.

Lastly, mental health is a pivotal aspect of both parenting and child development. Recognizing the signs of mental health issues, prioritizing self-care, and maintaining open lines of communication will ensure both you and your children are equipped to handle emotional struggles effectively.

This book aims to provide a comprehensive guide, weaving together scientific research, practical advice, and motivational insights. As we journey through the various facets of modern parenting, your unique experiences and intuition will be your best guides. Parenting is an evolving journey that requires adaptability, love, and a commitment to continual learning. Together, we'll explore the many paths to nurturing fulfilled and resilient children, empowering you to make choices that resonate with your values and circumstances.

In embracing the evolution of parenting, let's strive to create environments where children feel understood, valued, and equipped to navigate the world with confidence and compassion. Welcome to the dynamic and rewarding world of modern parenting.

Chapter 1:
Understanding Parenting Styles

As we delve into the foundation of raising well-rounded children, it's crucial to grasp the various parenting styles and their distinct characteristics. The four classic types—authoritative, authoritarian, permissive, and uninvolved—each present unique philosophies and practices. Research has shown that these styles significantly impact children's development, affecting their social skills, academic performance, and emotional resilience (Baumrind, 1966). Understanding the core principles behind each approach empowers parents to reflect on their own methods, making informed choices that resonate with their family's values and goals. By continually assessing and adapting our parenting style, we not only foster a nurturing environment but also instill a strong sense of stability and well-being in our children (Darling & Steinberg, 1993).

The Four Classic Styles

Delving into the heart of parenting, we come across four classic styles that have stood the test of time: Authoritative, Authoritarian, Permissive, and Uninvolved. Each of these styles carries distinct characteristics, shaping how parents interact with their children and influence their development. Authoritative parenting blends warmth and structure, promoting healthy independence while maintaining clear guidelines. In stark contrast, Authoritarian parenting emphasizes obedience and discipline, often at the expense of open communication and emotional connection. Permissive parenting, known for its leniency, allows children significant freedom but can sometimes lead to a lack of boundaries. Lastly, Uninvolved parenting, characterized by minimal engagement, may result in children feeling neglected and unsupported. Understanding these classic styles provides a foundational framework for caregivers to assess and refine their own approaches, ultimately fostering environments where children can thrive (Baumrind, 1991; Maccoby & Martin, 1983; Darling & Steinberg, 1993).

Authoritative Parenting is frequently held up as the gold standard when it comes to effective parenting styles. It represents a harmonious blend of demandingness and responsiveness. This approach balances setting high expectations for children while also providing them with the resources, support, and love they need to succeed. Esteemed psychologists like Diana Baumrind, who pioneered the theory of parenting styles, consider authoritative parenting as a robust means of promoting a child's emotional stability, academic success, and social competence (Baumrind, 1991).

One of the hallmarks of authoritative parenting is the establishment of clear, consistent rules and guidelines. These rules are explained in ways that children can understand. Instead of dictating behavior through an iron fist, authoritative parents believe in guiding their children through open dialogue and reasoning. This helps children internalize moral standards and develop a keen sense of right and wrong. As a result, they are less likely to exhibit behavioral problems and more likely to excel academically and socially (Steinberg, 2001).

Another key characteristic of authoritative parents is their responsiveness. They listen attentively to their children's needs and concerns, fostering an atmosphere of mutual respect. This responsive approach encourages children to communicate openly, thus building a healthy relationship based on trust. Authoritative parents are also known for being involved in their children's lives and showing keen interest in their activities, which contributes significantly to the child's sense of self-worth and confidence (Maccoby & Martin, 1983).

It's important to point out that authoritative parenting doesn't mean leniency or a lack of discipline. On the contrary, it includes well-defined boundaries and consequences for breaking rules. However, these consequences are logical and fair, providing an educational as well as a corrective experience for the child. This method of discipline ensures that children understand the repercussions of their actions, helping them develop a strong internal framework for managing their behavior as they grow (Baumrind, 1991).

Recent research supports the idea that authoritative parenting is highly effective across different cultures and settings. A study that observed diverse families found that children reared by authoritative parents exhibited higher levels of academic achievement and emotional well-being compared to those raised by parents employing other styles (Steinberg, 2001). This indicates that while cultural nuances exist, the core principles of authoritative parenting transcend cultural boundaries, making it a universally beneficial approach.

In the context of emotional development, authoritative parenting shines brightly. Children who grow up with authoritative parents tend to have higher levels of emotional intelligence. This is due to the environment of open communication and emotional support that authoritative parents cultivate. These children learn to navigate complex emotional landscapes, understand their own emotions better, and develop empathy towards others. All these are critical skills for forming healthy relationships later in life (Rinaldi & Howe, 2012).

Given the positive outcomes, many parents may wonder how to adopt and maintain an authoritative parenting style. First and foremost, it requires a commitment to being both firm and loving. This means setting high expectations but also providing the necessary support to meet those expectations. It also involves a consistent effort to be responsive to a child's needs, encouraging open dialogue and fostering a nurturing environment where the child feels valued and understood.

This approach is not without its challenges. Being an authoritative parent requires time and patience. It demands a deeper level of engagement, as you need to explain rules and expectations clearly, listen to your children's viewpoints, and negotiate solutions that take both the parents' and the child's perspectives into account. However, the long-term benefits make it a worthy investment (Maccoby & Martin, 1983).

Moreover, authoritative parents are adept at balancing flexibility with consistency. They are willing to adjust rules and expectations in response to a child's growing maturity and changing circumstances. For example, a curfew might be extended as a youngster demonstrates responsible behavior. This flexibility doesn't mean an abandonment of principles but rather an adaptive strategy to help the child develop autonomy and self-regulation (Rinaldi & Howe, 2012).

One area where authoritative parenting has shown significant impact is in academic success. Research indicates that children raised by authoritative parents tend to have a greater interest in learning and higher academic achievements. This success is attributed to the supportive environment that fosters curiosity, independence, and intrinsic motivation. Authoritative parents encourage their children to solve problems on their own, praise their efforts, and support them through challenges, thereby fostering a love of learning that lasts a lifetime (Steinberg, 2001).

Interestingly, authoritative parenting also mitigates the negative effects of stress on children. Due to the strong emotional bonds and open communication, children feel more secure and supported. They are more likely to turn to their parents for guidance during stressful times, which helps buffer the impact of stress and promotes resilience. This emotional safety net is crucial for healthy psychological development (Rinaldi & Howe, 2012).

In summary, **Authoritative Parenting** represents the epitome of balanced parenting. It effectively combines high expectations with substantial emotional support. This style not only promotes good behavior and academic success but also fosters a child's emotional and psychological well-being. While it requires effort, the payoff is substantial, making it a highly recommended approach for parents seeking to raise well-rounded, resilient, and successful children.

Authoritarian Parenting can be a word that stirs a mix of emotions for both parents and children. Grounded in a traditional, hierarchical approach, this style of parenting demands high expectations and strict adherence to rules. Renowned for its rigidity, authoritarian parenting leaves little room for negotiation or flexibility. While some parents may believe it instills discipline and respect, others argue that its excessive control can stifle a child's individual development and self-esteem.

Originating from the early 20th-century psychological theories, authoritarian parenting has been described extensively in the works of developmental psychologists like Diana Baumrind. Baumrind (1966) characterized it as a pattern where parents exhibit high demands but offer low responsiveness. Essentially, parents following this style expect obedience without question and tend not to explain the reasoning behind their rules. The rationale is often, "Because I said so," which can become a recurring mantra in authoritarian households. This approach leaves little room for a child to voice their opinions or make choices, positioning the parent as the central authority figure and limiting opportunities for open dialogue.

When we examine the implications of authoritarian parenting, the psychological impacts on children come into sharp focus. Studies have shown that children raised in such environments may develop a variety of emotional and behavioral issues. According to research, these children are more prone to exhibit signs of anxiety and depression (Gershoff et al., 2010). They might also struggle with self-esteem, having been conditioned to believe that their thoughts and feelings are less important or, worse, invalid. This can lead to a lack of self-confidence, as they are less likely to trust their own judgment when they are constantly told what to do.

The academics behind this perspective argue that the authoritarian style can also impede the development of critical social skills. For instance, children who are not allowed to question or negotiate may find themselves poorly equipped to engage in constructive social interactions outside their home. This can manifest in difficulties forming friendships or expressing themselves appropriately in social settings. Over time, this can hinder their ability to build and maintain healthy interpersonal relationships, which is a crucial aspect of overall well-being.

Nevertheless, it would be unfair to paint authoritarian parenting entirely in a negative light without acknowledging its potential benefits. For one, this style does establish clear expectations and boundaries, which can provide a structured environment that some children might thrive in. In scenarios where predictability and routine are vital, such as households dealing with chaotic external factors, authoritarian parenting can offer a sense of stability and security. This perspective was highlighted by Steinberg (2001), who pointed out that a structured environment could occasionally benefit children dealing with high-stress conditions.

However, the balancing act lies in implementing rules without suppressing a child's autonomy. Parents who lean towards an authoritarian style might benefit from incorporating certain elements of authoritative parenting – another style discussed alongside authoritarian in Baumrind's framework. The authoritative approach, characterized by high responsiveness paired with high demands, can create a more nurturing environment while still maintaining discipline. Parents can set clear rules but also explain the reasons behind them, invite dialogue, and offer support when needed. This hybrid approach can foster a more balanced developmental environment for children, encouraging both discipline and independence.

It's crucial to understand that authoritarian parenting doesn't exist in a vacuum; it often reflects the broader socio-cultural context. Cultural norms play a significant role in shaping parenting practices. In many Eastern cultures, where collectivism prevails and family hierarchy is deeply ingrained, authoritarian parenting might be more accepted and even expected. In contrast, Western cultures, which often emphasize individuality and democratic family structures, may view this style as overly rigid and potentially harmful. These cultural nuances add layers of complexity to the discussion, demonstrating that what might be viewed as "authoritarian" in one context could be seen as routine or even beneficial in another (Chao, 1994).

The cross-cultural perspective provides a nuanced understanding of why parents might adopt authoritarian methods. For instance, parents from immigrant backgrounds might hold on to this style as part of their cultural identity, striving to instill the values they grew up with in their children. However, for such parents, blending the positive aspects of their traditional practices with more modern, responsive techniques might create a more adaptive parenting style suited to their bicultural reality.

The effects of authoritarian parenting extend into various aspects of a child's life, including their academic performance and their ability to navigate challenges independently. Researchers have found a correlation between authoritarian parenting and academic outcomes. Children raised under strict, consistent rules tend to perform well academically in the short term due to their disciplined approach. However, the long-term effects can be less favorable. These children might fare poorly in environments that require critical thinking, creativity, or problem-solving skills – areas where a more autonomous upbringing may give other children an edge (Steinberg et al., 1992).

In the context of problem-solving, children from authoritarian households might lack initiative. Having been trained to follow instructions passively, they may struggle when asked to think independently or come up with innovative solutions. This can impact their performance in higher education and their professional lives, where such skills are often crucial.

Despite its challenges, transitioning from an authoritarian to a more balanced parenting style is possible and can have profound benefits. Integrating practices that encourage open communication and validation can help bridge the gap. Start by offering children choices in their daily activities, allowing them to feel a sense of control and responsibility. Additionally, take time to explain the reasons behind rules and decisions. This not only helps children understand the logic but also shows them that their parents respect their intellectual capacity.

In conclusion, while authoritarian parenting has its downfalls, it also offers a lesson in the importance of structure and discipline. The goal isn't to dismiss it entirely but to adapt its strengths into a more responsive, nurturing framework. As modern parents aiming to raise well-rounded individuals, the key lies in finding that sweet spot where structure meets understanding, discipline meets dialogue, and authority meets empathy. Balancing these elements can pave the way for healthier, happier, and more resilient children who are equipped to navigate life's complexities with confidence and competence.

Permissive Parenting is often characterized by high responsiveness but low demands. This parenting style, distinguished by leniency and a nurturing attitude, allows children considerable freedom to make their own decisions. The core idea is to be loving and involved while placing minimal demands on a child's behavior or household responsibilities (Baumrind, 1991). But what does this mean for your family, and how can it shape a child's development? Let's dig in and understand this further.

Permissive parents are known for their warm and accepting demeanor. They tend to avoid confrontation and are forgiving, often accepting a child's behavior without showing much disapproval (Maccoby & Martin, 1983). They are more likely to serve a friend-like role rather than an authoritative one. This is not to say they don't care about their children's behavior; they just prioritize creating a positive emotional climate over demanding conformity and obedience.

Such a parenting style might result in children who are well-adjusted emotionally because they grow up feeling loved and accepted. But, it's essential to acknowledge that balance is crucial. Without enough boundaries or expectations, children may struggle with self-discipline and self-regulation skills, facing difficulties in settings where rules and norms are essential, such as school or social environments.

A potential pitfall of permissive parenting is that it can cultivate a sense of entitlement in children. When parents rarely say "no," children might develop unrealistic expectations about receiving their desires without effort. This can translate into adult behaviors that are less resilient and more prone to frustration when faced with challenges or limitations (Baumrind, 1978).

Moreover, permissive parenting can inadvertently lead to an inconsistency that confuses children. While one's emotional support is crucial, the absence of rules or guidance can leave children feeling adrift. Effective boundaries provide a sense of security and help children understand the consequences of their actions (Baumrind, 1991). Studies suggest that a lack of such boundaries can result in behavioral issues, such as defiance and aggressiveness (Baumrind, 1978).

On the flip side, permissive parenting has its benefits. Children are encouraged to explore their creativity and independence. They often become strong in their sense of self and are more likely to pursue their passions without feeling constrained by rigid expectations. This style can foster strong parent-child relationships, as children view their parents as allies rather than enforcers.

Scientific research supports a balanced view. Studies have shown that some degree of permissive behavior can be beneficial, provided it is complemented with enough structure to guide decision-making (Darling & Steinberg, 1993). A warm and nurturing atmosphere is critical, but rules and boundaries help set the framework within which children can safely explore and grow.

Implementing a permissive parenting approach can be experimentally verified through real-life practices. For example, allowing children to make choices about their daily activities, such as selecting what to wear or deciding their after-school schedule, empowers them with autonomy. At the same time, the parents can gently guide the child's choices by setting some non-negotiable limits that keep the child grounded.

In this context, permissive parenting doesn't mean neglecting parental duties. Instead, it's about striking the right balance between affectionate freedom and effective boundaries. Parents should strive to be responsive to their children's needs while also teaching them the importance of rules and limits for their well-being. To achieve this, parents can communicate openly about expectations and involve their children in the decision-making process, helping them understand the rationale behind certain rules.

Furthermore, talking to your children about the consequences of their actions, both positive and negative, enhances their ability to make informed decisions. For instance, explaining why it's important to complete homework helps children see the value in education and the benefits of being responsible. This kind of guided autonomy is the essence of effective permissive parenting.

Another essential aspect to consider is emotional coaching. Permissive parents can use their nurturing approach to teach emotional intelligence and empathy. They can help their children manage emotions, deal with stress, and navigate social relationships. These skills are crucial for personal development and long-term success (Gottman et al., 1997).

In conclusion, while permissive parenting involves being highly responsive and less demanding, the key to successful implementation lies in achieving harmony between affection and structure. By providing a loving and supportive environment and setting reasonable boundaries, parents can help their children develop into well-rounded individuals capable of facing life's challenges with resilience and confidence. If you resonate with the permissive style, remember that your role moves beyond just being a friend—it's also about being a wise guide.

Uninvolved Parenting is a term frequently used to describe a style of parenting that is characterized by a distinct lack of responsiveness to a child's needs. Unlike other parenting styles, such as authoritative or permissive, uninvolved parenting is notably marked by a general disengagement from a child's emotional and physical life. Parents who fall into this category often provide for basic needs such as food, shelter, and hygiene, but show minimal involvement in other aspects of the child's development such as education, hobbies, and social interactions.

It's crucial to understand that uninvolved parenting is not always a deliberate choice. In many cases, it's a consequence of external factors such as parental stress, economic challenges, or mental health issues. When parents are overwhelmed by their circumstances, their capacity to engage actively in their children's lives can be severely impeded. This neglect can inadvertently impact various aspects of a child's development, leading to long-term ramifications. Studies have shown that children raised by uninvolved parents often exhibit poor academic performance, diminished self-esteem, and socio-emotional difficulties (Bigner, 2018).

An important note here is that the anthropological roots of uninvolved parenting can be traced back to environments where survival took precedence over emotional bonding. In societies where resource scarcity was an issue, the primary focus of parenting was often on ensuring the child's basic survival needs. However, in modern contexts, uninvolved parenting is typically viewed as inadequate due to its lack of emotional support. Despite modern awareness, current global trends still see this style persisting in various intensities across different cultures (Lamb, 2012).

What does this mean for the child's psyche? The absence of a nurturing presence can lead to an array of learning and behavioral issues. Children who grow up in uninvolved homes often lack the fortified emotional framework needed to navigate life's challenges effectively. Emotional learning is stunted, leading to difficulties in forming healthy relationships later in life (Davidov & Grusec, 2006).

Uninvolved parenting might seem like a passive issue, but its implications are far-reaching. For one, there's the academic sphere. Research consistently indicates that children from uninvolved households perform poorly in school. They're more likely to drop out of high school and less likely to pursue higher education (Mandara, 2006). Without the emotional and academic encouragement typically provided by engaged parents, these children struggle to establish the intrinsic motivation necessary for educational success.

In an emotional context, the impact is even more pronounced. These children often grapple with feelings of neglect and abandonment, creating a cycle of low self-esteem and poor mental health outcomes. They may develop attachment issues, rendering them either overly dependent on others for validation or entirely self-reliant, shunning emotional connections (Davidov & Grusec, 2006). In extreme cases, children from uninvolved settings are at a higher risk for delinquent behavior and substance abuse as they seek external sources of validation and solace (Mandara & Murray, 2002).

So, what can be done if you recognize elements of uninvolved parenting in your own approach? Self-awareness is the first step. Acknowledging the issue and its potential impacts can catalyze change. Parents who find themselves leaning toward this style often benefit from external support. This might be in the form of parenting classes, financial assistance, or mental health services to address underlying stresses that contribute to their disengagement.

Building a supportive community is another crucial strategy. Engaging with other parents, family members, or even community activities can foster a richer, more supportive environment for both the parent and the child. Involvement in parenting groups and resource networks can provide external motivation and practical strategies to help parents become more engaged in their children's lives (Bigner, 2018).

Schools and educators can also play a pivotal role. They can offer programs that encourage parental involvement and help bridge the gap between home and educational environments. Regular communication between parents and teachers, participation in school events, and parental input into academic planning can make a significant difference in outcomes for children (Lamb, 2012).

For those who may struggle with time constraints due to work or other responsibilities, even small changes can yield positive effects. Simple activities like a family dinner, bedtime stories, or dedicated 'check-in' times can significantly enhance a child's sense of security and belonging. Active listening during these times can go a long way in making the child feel valued and understood.

In conclusion, while uninvolved parenting may arise out of various unavoidable circumstances, its impact on children can be profound and long-lasting. The key lies in recognizing the patterns and actively seeking ways to heighten parental engagement. By harnessing community support, engaging with educators, and making conscious efforts to spend quality time with their children, parents can transform an uninvolved dynamic into one characterized by warmth, support, and active involvement.

Making even small, consistent gestures can be the stepping stones toward cultivating a positive and nurturing environment. Understanding the far-reaching implications of uninvolved parenting—and taking active steps to address them—can help parents guide their children toward healthier, happier futures.

Chapter 2: The Impact of Culture on Parenting

Culture shapes our beliefs, behaviors, and values, significantly influencing how we approach parenting. Around the globe, the spectrum of parenting styles is as diverse as the cultures from which they derive. While Eastern parenting often emphasizes obedience, respect, and the collective harmony of the family, Western approaches frequently prioritize individuality, independence, and self-expression (Chao, 1994; Lim & Lim, 2003). This cultural divergence can impact not only the methods parents use but also their goals and expectations for their children's development. For instance, in communities where tradition holds strong sway, parents may rely on time-honored practices and community wisdom, while modernized societies might lean toward evidence-based strategies, likelier to adapt to new psychological insights (Bornstein, 2012). Ultimately, understanding the cultural context of parenting provides a nuanced perspective that can equip caregivers to blend beneficial elements from various traditions and modern approaches, all while fostering a nurturing atmosphere that supports their children's unique needs and potentials.

Eastern vs. Western Approaches

Parenting is deeply influenced by cultural contexts, and one of the most striking differences can be seen when comparing Eastern and Western approaches. These approaches vary in terms of values, expectations, and parenting methods. Understanding these differences can offer parents a richer perspective and enable them to borrow effective strategies from both traditions.

One of the most prominent differences between Eastern and Western parenting is the emphasis on collectivism versus individualism. Eastern cultures, particularly those across Asia, often prioritize the group over the individual. In these cultures, children are raised with a strong sense of filial piety, respect for elders, and community responsibility (Chao, 1994). This collective mindset encourages children to think of their actions in the context of family and social harmony.

Western parenting, particularly in the United States and parts of Europe, tends to emphasize individualism. Here, the focus is often on nurturing a child's unique talents and self-expression. Parents encourage autonomy and self-reliance, preparing children to become independent adults who can stand on their own (Triandis, 1995). This approach fosters a sense of personal responsibility and freedom but can sometimes lead to challenges in instilling a sense of community and interdependence.

Discipline methods also vary significantly between these cultural paradigms. Eastern parenting often employs more authoritarian techniques, emphasizing obedience and respect for authority (Chen & Eisenberg, 2012). Strict discipline, academic excellence, and adherence to family rules are often stressed. For example, Chinese "Tiger Moms" may impose rigorous study schedules and have high academic expectations. This approach, while potentially leading to high achievement, can sometimes cause stress and inhibit creativity.

In contrast, Western parenting styles, particularly authoritative parenting, balance nurturing with setting boundaries. Parents are more likely to adopt a democratic style, involving children in decision-making and setting rules through discussion and mutual agreement

(Baumrind, 1991). This approach aims to develop critical thinking and self-regulation while maintaining a warm and supportive family environment. However, critics argue that it can sometimes lead to permissiveness and a lack of discipline.

Educational aspirations in Eastern versus Western cultures also reflect these differing philosophies. In many Asian cultures, education is seen as the primary route to success, and there is often intense pressure on children to excel academically (Stevenson & Stigler, 1992). The school system and the family's expectations create a rigorous daily routine focused on study and academic achievement.

Western approaches to education tend to promote a broader development of skills, including extracurricular activities and social skills. This holistic approach encourages a balance between academic pursuits and personal interests. While it fosters well-rounded development, it can sometimes result in less academic rigor compared to Eastern practices (Nguyen & Ryan, 2008).

Another notable difference is the role of parental involvement. In Eastern cultures, parents, particularly mothers, are often deeply involved in every aspect of their children's lives, from academics to personal decisions. This high level of involvement can create a strong safety net but may also limit children's ability to make independent choices.

In contrast, Western parents are more likely to encourage independence from a young age. Children are taught to make their own decisions, solve their problems, and learn from their experiences. This type of upbringing fosters self-confidence and problem-solving skills but may sometimes leave children feeling unsupported in times of need (Pomerantz et al., 2011).

The differences between Eastern and Western parenting are also evident in the way parents perceive and respond to their children's achievements and failures. Eastern parents often emphasize effort and perseverance, encouraging their children to view challenges as opportunities for growth. This mindset can foster resilience and a strong work ethic but can also contribute to significant pressure and stress.

Western parents, on the other hand, often emphasize the importance of self-esteem and personal fulfillment. They are more likely to praise their children's efforts and successes openly and may adopt a more relaxed attitude toward failures, viewing them as part of the learning process. This approach can foster a positive self-image and confidence but may sometimes result in lower academic pressure (Heine et al., 2001).

While these generalizations highlight key distinctions, it's important to recognize that parenting styles are on a spectrum and influenced by many factors, including socioeconomic status, education, and personal experiences. Moreover, globalization and cross-cultural exchange are blurring these distinctions. Parents worldwide are increasingly exposed to diverse parenting philosophies and are adopting hybrid approaches that combine elements from different cultures (Bornstein, 2012).

The challenge for parents lies in striking a balance between these differing approaches. Borrowing elements from both Eastern and Western traditions can create a more nuanced and flexible parenting style. For instance, Western parents can benefit from incorporating the Eastern emphasis on respect and discipline, ensuring their children understand the importance of hard work and community. Similarly, Eastern parents might adopt Western techniques that promote individuality and emotional expression, helping their children develop confidence and independent thinking.

Ultimately, there is no one-size-fits-all approach to parenting. The key is to remain adaptable and responsive to the unique needs of each child, drawing on the strengths of both Eastern and Western traditions. By doing so, parents can foster an environment that nurtures their children's growth, resilience, and well-being.

The Influence of Tradition and Modernity

Tradition and modernity represent the dual forces that shape our collective understanding of parenting, juxtaposing long-standing customs with contemporary practices. In a world that's evolving at a rapid pace, the clash and fusion of these two paradigms have significant implications for parenting styles. This delicate balance between respecting cultural heritage and embracing new methodologies shapes how children are raised and how parents navigate their responsibilities.

Consider the traditional communities that value age-old practices, often handed down through generations, as the cornerstone of raising children. These practices are rooted in historical contexts, societal norms, and familial structures that emphasize values like obedience, respect for authority, and collective responsibility. For instance, in many Eastern societies, the Confucian philosophy deeply influences parenting, promoting harmony, filial piety, and a hierarchy within the family structure (Chao, 1994). These principles have withstood the test of time, ingrained in the culture and psyche of the people.

On the other end of the spectrum, modernity brings with it a wave of liberal philosophies and scientific advancements, advocating for more individualistic approaches. The rise of psychology and child development theories in the Western world has shifted the focus toward understanding the child as an individual with unique needs and rights. Concepts such as positive reinforcement, child-led learning, and emotional intelligence are gaining traction, encouraging parents to adopt practices that foster independence and self-regulation (Baumrind, 1991).

In blending tradition with modernity, parents find themselves in a dynamic interplay of values and methodologies. This fusion isn't about choosing one over the other; instead, it's about creating a hybrid approach that respects cultural identities while adapting to the contemporary world. For example, authoritative parenting, which blends high responsiveness with high demands, can be seen as a modern twist on traditional authoritative approaches, incorporating nurturing aspects alongside discipline (Baumrind, 1966).

The tension between these paradigms also reflects in the way community and collectivism are perceived versus individualism and personal achievement. Traditional approaches often emphasize community and extended family involvement in child-rearing, providing a broader support system. In contrast, modern approaches might focus more on the nuclear family's role, with an emphasis on personal growth and self-sufficiency. This dichotomy does not necessarily have to be a source of conflict; instead, it presents an opportunity for integrating broader support networks while fostering personal responsibility in children.

Educational practices also highlight this blending of tradition and modernity. In many cultures, traditional education emphasizes rote learning and discipline, aiming to cultivate respect and perseverance. Modern educational philosophies like the Montessori method or Reggio Emilia approach prioritize experiential learning, creativity, and critical thinking skills. Parents who navigate these worlds might opt for an educational environment that upholds some traditional values while incorporating modern pedagogical techniques.

It's important to note that the decision to adhere to tradition or embrace modernity often isn't solely within a parent's control. Socio-economic factors, access to education, and exposure to global cultures significantly impact these choices. In many developing nations, economic constraints may force parents to rely more heavily on traditional methods, whereas in more affluent settings, parents might have the luxury to experiment with different styles informed by the latest research.

Moreover, the digital age has profoundly affected this dynamic. Technology creates avenues for modern parenting strategies to disseminate globally, providing access to a wealth of information and parenting resources. Yet, it simultaneously challenges traditional ways of familial communication and bonding. Parents are now tasked with integrating digital literacy into their child's upbringing while managing screen time and online safety—issues that were non-existent in the traditional paradigms.

On a more personal level, parents also bring their personalities, beliefs, and experiences into their parenting style, making each approach unique. Some parents may find comfort and security in traditional practices that resonate with their upbringing, while others may be more inclined to forge new paths based on modern understandings of child development. This personal blend of tradition and modernity creates a unique parenting tapestry, reflective of individual and cultural identities.

The mental health of both parents and children is another critical area where tradition and modernity intersect. Traditional approaches may sometimes overlook the importance of mental health, focusing primarily on physical well-being and societal roles. Modern parenting, on the other hand, tends to be more holistic, acknowledging the need for mental and emotional support as integral to healthy development. Integrating mental well-being practices into traditional frameworks can create a more balanced and supportive environment for children.

Ultimately, the influence of tradition and modernity on parenting is a testament to the adaptability and resilience of families worldwide. By understanding the strengths and limitations of both paradigms, parents can craft an enriched parenting experience that prepares their children to thrive in a multifaceted world. Embracing this duality allows for a harmonious blend that respects the past while eagerly stepping into the future, equipped with the best tools and insights available.

In recognizing the dynamic interplay between these forces, it's evident that there's no one-size-fits-all approach to parenting. Each culture offers valuable lessons, and borrowing from both traditional and modern practices can create a more robust, well-rounded approach to raising children. As parents and caregivers, the aim should be to remain open and flexible, continuously learning and adapting to provide the best possible foundation for the next generation.

By striking this balance, parents can honor their heritage while fostering environments conducive to growth, innovation, and emotional well-being. This holistic approach ensures that children are not only prepared to navigate the complexities of the modern world but also deeply rooted in their cultural identities, providing them with a sense of belonging and purpose.

Chapter 3:
The Role of Gender in Parenting Practices

In the evolving landscape of modern parenting, the role of gender has become a significant variable influencing parenting practices. Traditionally, gender roles have dictated that mothers are the nurturers while fathers are the providers. However, contemporary research and societal shifts question these rigid stereotypes, suggesting instead a more fluid approach to parenting responsibilities. Studies show that when both parents engage equally in nurturing and disciplinary roles, children benefit from a well-rounded emotional and cognitive development (Lamb, 2010). Furthermore, embracing a flexible approach to gender roles in parenting can foster a sense of equality and mutual respect in the household, setting a powerful example for children to emulate in their social interactions and future relationships (Pleck, 2012). When fathers take on caregiving roles and mothers participate in activities traditionally reserved for fathers, it helps dismantle outdated gender norms and promotes a more inclusive environment for children to grow up in. This shift not only aids in the healthy development of children but also enhances the fulfillment and dynamics within the family unit (Parke, 2013).

Challenging Gender Stereotypes

In the journey of parenting, confronting and dismantling gender stereotypes is one of the most impactful steps you can take. From the moment a child is born, societal expectations start shaping their identity and behavior based on their gender. These conventional roles dictate how boys and girls should act, what they should be interested in, and how they are supposed to engage with the world. But do these stereotypes hold any real value? Scientific research suggests that breaking free from these constraints can lead to healthier and more balanced development for children (Witt, 2000).

Let's start by addressing the early years of child-rearing. Often, the toys we buy, the colors we choose, and the activities we encourage are heavily influenced by gender norms. Pink for girls, blue for boys. Dolls for daughters, trucks for sons. While this seems harmless, it's crucial to realize that such practices can define children's perceptions of their roles in society from a very young age. Studies show that children who are allowed to explore a wide range of activities and interests, regardless of gender, are more likely to develop a richer array of skills and a more well-rounded personality (Sullivan, 2013).

Now, let's dive into the realm of emotional expression. Historically, boys are taught to be tough, hide their feelings, and strive for dominance, while girls are encouraged to be nurturing, empathetic, and expressive. This binary can stifle both genders. A boy who is discouraged from showing emotion may grow into an adult who struggles with vulnerability and interpersonal connections. On the flip side, a girl who is overly shielded from competitive environments may lack the assertiveness needed to seize opportunities. Breaking these molds can pave the way for children to grow into emotionally intelligent adults, capable of both empathy and assertiveness (Brody, 1999).

Marriage and co-parenting further complicate how gender roles affect parenting practices. Traditional roles often designate mothers as the primary caregivers and fathers as the breadwinners. However, this dynamic is changing, and for good reason. Research indicates that a balanced division of labor between parents can lead to better outcomes for the entire family. When fathers are equally involved in child-rearing, children benefit from a broader spectrum of emotional, social, and cognitive growth (Lamb, 2004). Likewise, when mothers engage in the workforce, they often serve as strong role models for both their sons and daughters, showcasing that careers are not bound by gender.

Challenging stereotypes within the family structure is not just about reversing roles; it's about fluidity and flexibility. It's about allowing both parents to develop a deep emotional bond with their children and share the workload, whether physical or emotional. This sets a positive example for children, showing them that both men and women can be nurturing, strong, and competent providers.

Another critical area where gender stereotypes play out is in education and extracurricular activities. Boys are often pushed toward STEM (science, technology, engineering, and mathematics), while girls are steered towards the humanities and arts. This divide has long-term consequences on children's career choices and their self-perception of their abilities. In the U.S., for instance, women constitute only 28% of the STEM workforce (National Science Board, 2018). Encouraging children to explore subjects and activities outside traditional gender roles can help balance this disparity, fostering a generation that is both more innovative and inclusive.

Additionally, the portrayal of gender roles in media and popular culture can't be ignored. Television, movies, and books often reinforce traditional gender norms, presenting a challenge for parents who are trying to raise children free from these constraints. It's important to curate the content your children consume and have open discussions about the stereotypes they encounter. By doing so, you can help them develop critical thinking skills and a more nuanced understanding of identity.

One might wonder, how do we practically apply these concepts in daily life? Start with small but meaningful changes. Introduce a variety of toys, books, and activities to your children. Encourage them to pursue their interests, whether they align with traditional gender roles or not. When your son wants to dance or your daughter wants to build a robot, show them that their interests are valid and celebrated. Actively participate in these activities with them, showing your support and enthusiasm.

In your interactions, be mindful of the language you use. Avoid phrases like "boys will be boys" or "that's not ladylike." These phrases reinforce the very stereotypes we aim to dismantle. Instead, emphasize traits like kindness, courage, and curiosity, which are valuable regardless of gender.

Let's also consider the broader societal structures that uphold these stereotypes. Schools, workplaces, and community organizations need to foster environments that challenge and change these outdated notions. As parents and caregivers, advocating for inclusive policies and practices can make a significant impact. Whether it's pushing for diverse representation in school curricula or fighting for parental leave policies that support both mothers and fathers, community efforts can bring about meaningful change.

Support systems and peer networks also play a vital role in this transformation. Parents' groups and community forums are excellent platforms to discuss experiences, exchange ideas, and gain support for raising children free from gender biases. These networks can serve as incubators for progress, providing resources and encouragement for parents committed to challenging the status quo.

In conclusion, the impact of confronting and overturning gender stereotypes is profound. Children raised in environments that shatter these norms tend to be more adaptable, empathetic, and equipped to deal with the complexities of modern society. They learn to appreciate each other for who they are rather than what society expects them to be. This is not merely a parenting choice; it is a social imperative that contributes to a more equitable and just world. By taking these steps, you are not only enhancing your child's development but also contributing to a larger movement towards gender equality and human potential.

So, what's holding you back? Dive into this journey of challenging gender stereotypes with enthusiasm and commitment. Your efforts today will pave the way for a brighter, more inclusive future.

Shaping Identity: Mothers and Fathers

Parents often find themselves navigating the complex waters of shaping their children's identities. In this transformative journey, mothers and fathers play pivotal roles, each bringing unique strengths and influences to the table. While it's easy to get lost in traditional roles defined by societal norms, acknowledging and embracing the diverse capabilities of both parents can lead to holistic, well-rounded development for the child.

Historically, mothers have been seen as the primary caregivers, responsible for nurturing and emotional support. Research has shown that maternal involvement is crucial for a child's emotional and social development (Bowlby, 1988). Mothers often serve as their children's first teachers, demonstrating empathy and understanding through everyday interactions. The nurturing environment provided by a mother can lay the foundation for emotional intelligence, teaching children how to recognize and manage their own emotions effectively.

On the other hand, fathers have traditionally been viewed as providers and protectors. However, this narrow view fails to capture the richness of paternal contributions. Studies indicate that fathers who are engaged in their children's lives contribute positively to their cognitive, social, and emotional well-being (Pleck & Masciadrelli,

2004). When fathers participate actively, they model behaviors such as problem-solving, resilience, and independence. These interactions teach children essential life skills and prepare them to face real-world challenges confidently.

It is essential to consider the evolving dynamics of family structures in today's world. With more dual-income households and diverse family arrangements, traditional gender roles are continuously being redefined. Parents must work in tandem, sharing responsibilities and adapting to their unique family context. For example, stay-at-home dads are becoming increasingly common, and their active involvement has been shown to have substantial benefits. The flexibility to interchange roles allows children to see both parents as equal partners, promoting a balanced perspective on gender roles.

Parents should also understand the impact of their own gender identities on their children. Children learn by observing the behavior, attitudes, and interactions of their parents. If they see gender equality and mutual respect in their household, they're more likely to emulate those values. Breaking free from rigid stereotypes allows children to explore their own identities without the constraints of traditional gender expectations.

It's important to foster open communication within the family. Encouraging dialogue about gender, roles, and identities helps children feel more secure in expressing themselves. Parents should support their children's exploration of interests and talents, providing a nurturing environment that celebrates diversity. Whether a daughter shows interest in science or a son in cooking, it's the parents' acceptance and encouragement that will empower their children to pursue their passions without fear of judgment.

The balancing act between mothers and fathers becomes even more significant considering the societal pressures and cultural expectations that still persist. Some parents might grapple with external judgments when stepping outside traditional roles. However, it's imperative to prioritize the emotional and developmental needs of the child above societal norms. By doing so, parents can create a nurturing environment conducive to growth, learning, and self-discovery.

Moreover, it's crucial to acknowledge that parenting does not occur in a vacuum. Each parent brings their own life experiences, cultural background, and personal strengths to the table. Fathers may offer unique perspectives shaped by their own upbringing, while mothers might provide insights drawn from different experiences. This blend of viewpoints enriches the parenting approach, offering children a broad spectrum of guidance and wisdom.

Additionally, mindfulness in parenting practices cannot be overstated. Being present and attuned to the child's needs and feelings, irrespective of whether you're a mother or a father, fosters a secure and trusting relationship. Active listening, shared activities, and consistent support provide the cornerstone for a child's healthy identity formation. These practices are universal and transcend any gendered expectations.

In moments of doubt or challenge, leveraging support systems can make a significant difference. Full cooperation between mothers and fathers, combined with the advice and support of extended family, parenting groups, or professional resources, can equip parents with the tools they need. Each situation is unique, and sometimes external perspectives can bring clarity and innovative solutions to complex problems.

Finally, remember that parenting is an evolving journey. Both mothers and fathers need to remain adaptable, open to learning, and willing to grow alongside their children. The fluid exchange of roles and responsibilities enriches the parental partnership, offering a dynamic and supportive environment where children can thrive. By consciously shaping their approach to parenting with love, respect, and open-mindedness, mothers and fathers can pave the way for their children to develop into confident, well-rounded individuals.

Chapter 4: Attachment Theory and Parenting

Understanding attachment theory is vital for parents wishing to foster healthy, lasting bonds with their children. At its core, attachment theory posits that the quality of the early relationship between a child and their primary caregiver fundamentally shapes the child's development and future relationships (Bowlby, 1988). Secure attachments, characterized by a caregiver's responsiveness and availability, lead to children who are more resilient, empathetic, and emotionally balanced (Ainsworth et al., 1978). Conversely, insecure attachments, which may arise from inconsistent or neglectful caregiving, can result in anxiety, difficulty in relationships, and emotional dysregulation (Cassidy & Shaver, 2016). It is crucial for parents to recognize the signs of secure and insecure attachments and employ practical strategies—like consistent emotional support and positive reinforcement—to build strong, healthy bonds. By doing so, parents not only nurture a secure base for their children to explore the world but also equip them with the essential skills to navigate life's challenges.

Secure and Insecure Attachments

Understanding the concept of secure and insecure attachments is vital for parents striving to foster a nurturing environment. These attachment types form the foundation of a child's relationships and emotional well-being. Secure attachments create confident, resilient individuals who can handle life's ups and downs effectively. On the other hand, insecure attachments may lead to anxiety, trust issues, and challenges in social interactions.

But where do these attachments originate, and how do they develop? Attachment theory, first introduced by John Bowlby, posits that the bonds formed between a child and their caregiver critically impact the child's psychological development. A secure attachment develops when a caregiver consistently meets the child's needs with sensitivity, providing a reliable base of support (Ainsworth, 1979). Contrastingly, insecure attachments form when caregivers are inconsistent, unavailable, or unresponsive.

Secure attachments are characterized by several key behaviors and feelings. Children with secure attachments feel safe exploring their environment, knowing they can return to their caregiver for comfort and reassurance. They exhibit fewer behavioral problems, have better social relationships, and display higher emotional intelligence. This sense of security stems from having a caregiver who is attuned to their emotional state and can respond appropriately.

Insecure attachments can be divided further into avoidant, ambivalent, and disorganized attachments. Children with avoidant attachments tend to distance themselves emotionally from their caregivers. They have learned that their caregivers are not a reliable source of comfort or support. You might notice these children becoming exceedingly self-reliant at a young age but struggling with intimacy and trust later in life.

Ambivalent attachments arise when the caregiver is unpredictably responsive. Sometimes, the child's needs are met, and other times, they are ignored. This inconsistency leads to anxiety and uncertainty about whether their caregiver will be available. These children often appear clingy and overly dependent, struggling to feel secure.

Disorganized attachments are perhaps the most troubling and complex. These attachments often emerge in environments where the child experiences trauma, abuse, or caregivers who exhibit erratic behaviors. Children with disorganized attachments display a lack of clear attachment strategy. Their actions might seem unpredictable, and they often find it difficult to regulate their emotions or form coherent relationships.

Considering the significance of secure attachments, what strategies can parents use to nurture them? Firstly, emotional availability is crucial. Being present, both physically and emotionally, creates a foundation of trust. Active listening and validating your child's feelings, even when they can't articulate them well, show that you are attuned to their needs. It's not merely about spending time together but making sure that this time is enriching and reassuring (Siegel & Hartzell, 2003).

Routine and consistency also shelter a developing child. Predictable routines provide a sense of stability, helping them understand what to expect and when to expect it. This predictability reduces anxiety and fosters a sense of security. It's like building a solid home that is impervious to storms; the child knows they have a reliable refuge.

Another vital component is responsive caregiving. Infants and young children rely on their caregivers to help regulate emotions and stress. When a caregiver responds to a child's cries with patience, warmth, and appropriate intervention, the child learns effective emotional regulation. This responsiveness nurtures a secure attachment, showing the child that their caregiver is a dependable source of support (Cassidy & Shaver, 2016).

Mindful parenting principles can also bolster secure attachments. This involves being fully present during interactions with your child, paying attention to their cues, and responding empathetically.

Mindfulness helps parents remain calm and collected, even during challenging situations, minimizing the likelihood of overreactions that could contribute to insecure attachments.

Yet, despite best efforts, it's important to recognize that no parent is perfect. What matters most is consistency and the ability to repair breaches in attachment. When you make a mistake—as all parents do—acknowledge it and make amends. This process of rupture and repair reinforces the attachment bond and teaches your child about resilience and the importance of mending relationships.

In conclusion, understanding secure and insecure attachments equips parents with tools to build stronger, healthier relationships with their children. Fostering secure attachment starts with being emotionally available, consistent, and responsive. While the challenges are undeniable, the rewards are profound—confident, emotionally intelligent children who are well-prepared to navigate the complexities of life.

Practical Strategies for Building Strong Bonds

The foundation of a child's emotional and psychological development rests significantly on the bonds formed with their primary caregivers. Attachment theory underscores the importance of these early relationships, suggesting that the quality of the bond influences a child's ability to form secure relationships and cope with stress throughout life. So, what can parents and caregivers do to nurture these crucial connections effectively?

One of the foremost strategies is **responsive parenting**. This involves being attuned to your child's needs and responding to their emotional signals in a timely and appropriate manner. Studies indicate that children who experience consistent responsiveness are more likely to develop secure attachments (Ainsworth, 1979). For example, when a newborn cries, picking them up and soothing them not only addresses an immediate need but also lays the groundwork for trust. This doesn't stop at infancy; being attuned to a toddler's frustration or a teenager's anxiousness reinforces the same principle of emotional support.

Physical affection is another powerful way to build strong bonds. Hugs, kisses, and other forms of physical touch release oxytocin, often referred to as the "love hormone," which fosters a sense of well-being and emotional closeness. According to Field (2010), regular physical affection enhances the child's emotional health, leading to lower levels of anxiety and stress. Make it a habit to offer a comforting hug before school, a gentle back rub after a challenging day, or even a cuddle during a shared movie night.

Quality time is essential for developing strong attachments. It's not about the quantity but the quality of time spent with your children. Engage in activities that foster interaction rather than passive consumption, such as watching TV. Board games, craft projects, or even simple activities like cooking together can create emotionally enriching experiences. Moreover, these moments provide opportunities for parents to communicate values, share stories, and build mutual respect and understanding.

Sometimes, life's demands make it challenging to be present physically and emotionally. Here, **rituals and routines** can play a vital role. Establishing family traditions, whether it's a weekly game night, a morning breakfast ritual, or an annual holiday trip, can give children a sense of stability and security. These predictable elements in family life contribute to a child's sense of belonging and attachment (Fiese et al., 2002).

Open communication is critical. Encouraging your child to express their thoughts and feelings without fear of judgment creates a safe emotional environment. Active listening—wherein you truly hear what your child is saying, without interrupting or immediately providing solutions—validates their experiences and emotions. For instance, rather than dismissing a school-age child's worries about a friendship problem, acknowledging their feelings and discussing it openly can significantly strengthen your relationship.

In the digital age, **managing technology use** within the family is crucial to maintaining strong bonds. Establish screen-free times, particularly during meals or family gatherings, to ensure that these moments are reserved for face-to-face interaction. This doesn't mean cutting off technology entirely but striking a balance so that devices don't overshadow direct communication and relationship-building activities.

Another strategy lies in the **shared responsibilities and collaborative decision-making** within the family. Allowing children to have a say in family decisions that affect them fosters a sense of agency and supports emotional bonding. This could be as simple as choosing the menu for dinner or as significant as planning a family vacation. When children feel their opinions are valued, they are more likely to develop a secure attachment as they see themselves as integral members of the family unit.

For working parents who might struggle with time constraints, **bonding through daily tasks** can be highly effective. Turning mundane activities into special moments can make a significant difference. Whether it's grocery shopping, walking the dog, or preparing meals, these everyday tasks provide opportunities to talk, collaborate, and share experiences.

It's also essential to recognize the role of **positive reinforcement and encouragement**. Celebrate your child's achievements, no matter how small, to strengthen their confidence and reinforce your relationship. Positive reinforcement can be verbal praise, a special treat, or a small reward—anything that acknowledges their efforts and achievements.

Lastly, **modeling healthy relationships** within the family environment sets a strong example for children. Parents are role models, and the way they interact with each other, resolve conflicts, and show affection profoundly influences a child's perception of relationships. Healthy communication patterns, mutual respect, and demonstrating conflict resolution skills teach children how to form and maintain secure attachments in their own lives.

Incorporating these strategies into your parenting approach can transform the dynamics of your familial relationships. The key is consistency and genuine effort. When parents are proactive in fostering secure attachments, the benefits extend beyond childhood, preparing children to navigate life's challenges with resilience and emotional intelligence. By focusing on building strong, secure bonds, you're not just raising a child; you're nurturing a future adult capable of forming healthy, lasting relationships.

Chapter 5:
The Digital Age and Its Effect on Parental Guidance

In today's fast-paced digital era, parents face unique challenges and unprecedented opportunities in guiding their children. The omnipresence of technology—from smartphones and tablets to social media platforms—requires a new set of parenting skills that blend traditional wisdom with modern insights. On the one hand, digital tools can be harnessed to enhance education, creativity, and communication. On the other, they present risks such as screen addiction, cyberbullying, and exposure to inappropriate content. It's essential for parents to establish balanced screen time guidelines, encouraging meaningful interactions and offline activities. According to Common Sense Media, children aged 8-12 spend an average of six hours a day on digital media, highlighting the need for vigilant monitoring and open dialogues about online behavior (Common Sense Media, 2019). Additionally, it's crucial to equip children with critical thinking skills to navigate this complex landscape, fostering digital literacy and responsible usage. The digital age undeniably reshapes parental guidance, urging caregivers to adapt and evolve continuously to nurture well-rounded individuals.

Navigating Screen Time

As we've journeyed through the impact of the digital age on parenting, it's clear that screen time has become a monumental issue for families.

The question of how much is too much and what's appropriate for different age groups often weighs heavily on parents' minds. In an era dominated by tablets, smartphones, and computers, managing screen time requires both understanding and strategy.

One of the first aspects parents need to grasp is the nuanced nature of screen time. It's not just about the duration but also what kind of content is being consumed. Educational apps and programs can be beneficial, promoting literacy and cognitive skills. However, excessive video game playing or social media scrolling without positive engagement can have negative impacts on children's development (Anderson & Subrahmanyam, 2017).

Studies show that children aged 8 to 12 in the United States spend an average of 4 to 6 hours a day watching or using screens, while teens can spend up to 9 hours per day (Radesky et al., 2020). These figures can be alarming, but they also provide a starting point for establishing limits and guidelines. The American Academy of Pediatrics recommends no screen time (apart from video chatting) for children under 18 months, and for older children, it should be about creating a balanced approach (AAP, 2016).

Equipping children with self-regulation skills is essential in managing their screen use. This can be done by setting consistent rules and routines around screen time. For instance, implementing tech-free zones, like family meals and bedtime routines, encourages face-to-face interaction and better sleep hygiene. These small, steady habits foster a healthier relationship with technology.

A pivotal step in this digital age is leading by example. Children often mimic adults' behaviors, so it's crucial for parents to model balanced screen habits themselves. Demonstrating when and how technology should be used responsibly directly influences how children perceive and use their own devices. It's a practice grounded in modeling theory, which suggests that behaviors can be learned through the observation of others (Bandura, 1977).

Another layer to consider is the collaborative aspect of navigating screen time. It's beneficial when families discuss technology use openly, engage in digital activities together, and even co-view programs. This approach not only makes screen time a shared experience but also provides opportunities for parents to guide and educate children on critical thinking, cyber safety, and discernment in what they view online.

On a practical level, various tools can assist parents in mediating screen time. Parental control software, timers, and apps designed to limit usage periods can be effective in maintaining boundaries. However, reliance solely on technological solutions isn't sufficient; dialogue and understanding are key components of true screen time management.

It's also important to recognize that technology isn't inherently bad. It brings educational advancements, access to information, and connection to others around the globe. The challenge lies in managing its use wisely. Fostering digital literacy, where children learn to navigate online spaces safely and discerningly, is a critical skill. Encouraging them to think about the reasons behind their screen use can promote conscious engagement rather than mindless consumption.

One significant concern related to screen time is its correlation with physical activity and social interaction. Excessive screen use often replaces physical play and social experiences crucial for children's development. Encouraging outdoor activities, hobbies, and personal interests can serve as a counterbalance, promoting a well-rounded lifestyle.

Moreover, screen time isn't just a matter of physical health but mental and emotional well-being too. Overuse of screens, especially social media, can lead to issues like anxiety, depression, and feelings of isolation. Open communication about the emotions and experiences tied to digital interactions can help children process these feelings constructively. This conversation should be part of a broader discourse on emotional intelligence, helping children articulate and manage their emotions in various contexts.

With the increasing presence of screens, cybersecurity has become paramount. Teaching children about online privacy, the dangers of cyberbullying, and the importance of maintaining digital etiquette are essential components of responsible screen use. Creating a safe digital environment helps build trust and empowers children to make safer choices online.

Inside the home, creating a positive digital environment can also involve setting up spaces that separate learning and leisure activities. Designating particular areas for education helps in maintaining focus, while different zones dedicated to relaxation or recreation prevent these activities from blending into one another excessively.

One strategy to adopt is the "tech-break" mindset, a technique where certain times of the day are designated as screen-free. These breaks provide mental rest and encourage other activities, such as reading, crafts, or simply spending time with family. This balance fosters creativity, critical thinking, and a more active lifestyle.

Breaking the screen habit can be tough, but persistence pays off. Encourage rewards for screen-free activities, like extra playtime or a family outing. These incentives can motivate children to engage in offline experiences, gradually reducing their dependency on screens.

Finally, it's helpful to revisit and re-evaluate screen time rules periodically. As children grow and their needs change, so should the strategies for managing screen use. Regular check-ins allow families to adjust their approach, ensuring that guidelines remain relevant and effective.

In conclusion, navigating screen time isn't about adhering to rigid rules but finding equilibrium in a digital world. It's an ongoing journey of educating, modeling, and engaging with our children in meaningful ways. By establishing thoughtful, consistent habits and fostering open communication, parents can guide their children towards a healthier relationship with screens. This balance not only supports their development but also empowers them to thrive in a technologically rich environment.

Social Media: The Risks and Rewards

In our digital age, social media has become a double-edged sword, offering remarkable benefits while posing significant challenges for parents. Its reach is extensive, impacting the way children interact, learn, and develop. As parents and caregivers, understanding the nuances of social media can help guide children through its complexities while maximizing its benefits.

Firstly, let's discuss the rewards. Social media can be a powerful tool for learning and connecting. Educational content is abundant on platforms like YouTube, Instagram, and TikTok, where educational influencers, teachers, and even institutions worldwide provide free resources and tutorials. These channels can stimulate intellectual curiosity, enhance digital literacy, and offer real-time information on diverse subjects (Livingstone & Helsper, 2007). For parents, this presents an opportunity to supplement traditional education and foster a love for learning beyond the classroom.

Social media also offers a platform for social connections, especially crucial during times of social isolation. Sites like Facebook, WhatsApp, and Snapchat allow children to maintain friendships, engage in collaborative projects, and participate in group activities, even when physically distant. This connectivity can enhance social skills, promote teamwork, and even provide emotional support (Valkenburg et al., 2006). These positive interactions are vital for developing healthy social behaviors and emotional resilience.

However, the risks linked to social media are significant and cannot be ignored. One of the most pressing concerns is exposure to inappropriate content. Despite filters and parental controls, children can still encounter explicit or harmful material, impacting their mental and emotional well-being. This exposure can lead to distorted perceptions of reality, issues with self-esteem, and unhealthy comparisons with peers (Rideout et al., 2010).

Cyberbullying is another alarming risk associated with social media. The anonymity and reach of the internet can exacerbate traditional bullying, making it relentless and inescapable for victims. Cyberbullying can have severe consequences, including anxiety, depression, and in extreme cases, tragic outcomes like suicide. Parents must be vigilant, fostering open communication with their children about their online experiences and encouraging them to speak up about any bullying incidents (Kowalski et al., 2012).

Privacy concerns are also paramount. Children often share personal information online without understanding the potential repercussions. This can lead to identity theft, stalking, and other forms of online exploitation. Teaching children about the importance of privacy, how to manage their digital footprints, and the appropriate settings for social media accounts is essential for their online safety.

There's also the issue of screen addiction. Excessive use of social media can interfere with sleep, school performance, and physical activity, fostering a sedentary lifestyle. The constant need for validation through likes and comments can also lead to addictive behaviors, where children become overly reliant on online interactions for self-worth (Twenge et al., 2018). Balancing screen time with other activities is crucial for healthy development.

Parental guidance is pivotal in mitigating these risks. Establishing rules around social media use, such as setting time limits and monitoring activities, can help maintain a healthy balance. Encouraging children to engage in offline activities like sports, reading, or hobbies can provide a well-rounded lifestyle that doesn't revolve around screens.

Moreover, being a role model in social media use is essential. Children often emulate their parents' behaviors, so demonstrating responsible and balanced social media habits can set a positive example. Open discussions about the content they encounter online and fostering critical thinking can empower children to make informed decisions about their social media interactions.

Collaborating with educators and other parents is another effective strategy. Schools can play a crucial role in educating children about digital citizenship, the responsible use of technology, and the consequences of online actions. Parenting groups and online forums offer support and share practical tips on navigating the digital landscape, providing a community of collective wisdom and support.

Despite the challenges, the rewards of social media can be harnessed effectively with the right strategies. It offers unprecedented opportunities for learning, social connection, and personal growth. By approaching social media with vigilance, open communication, and a balanced perspective, parents can help their children reap its benefits while safeguarding against its risks.

Chapter 6:
Discipline and Setting Boundaries

Finding the right balance between discipline and freedom is a crucial aspect of effective parenting, impacting a child's development profoundly. Successful discipline requires a nuanced approach that adapts to the child's age and temperament, helping to instill values such as respect, responsibility, and self-control (Grolnick, 2012). Clear, consistent boundaries create a safe framework within which children can explore and grow, knowing their limits while also feeling secure (Baumrind, 1991). Rather than relying solely on punitive measures, parents can employ a combination of positive reinforcement and natural consequences to nurture intrinsic motivation and good behavior (Kazdin & Rotella, 2012). Remember, discipline is not about control, but about guiding children towards becoming well-rounded, emotionally intelligent individuals who understand the importance of boundaries in maintaining healthy relationships (Siegel & Bryson, 2014).

Effective Methods for Different Ages

When it comes to disciplining and setting boundaries, a one-size-fits-all approach simply won't do. Each developmental stage brings its own set of challenges and requires customized strategies tailored to the child's age. Understanding these nuances is essential for parents and caregivers who seek to foster discipline without compromising the child's emotional and psychological well-being.

Infants (0-2 years): Establishing Foundations

For infants, discipline is more about setting the groundwork for future discipline rather than direct corrective measures. At this age, babies are just beginning to understand the world and are heavily reliant on caregivers. Consistency is key. Establishing routines for feeding, sleeping, and play helps create a sense of security and predictability. This doesn't mean harsh rules but rather consistent patterns that help the infant understand what to expect (Siegel & Bryson, 2012).

Use gentle guidance and redirection rather than harsh disciplinary actions. For instance, if a baby starts to reach for something dangerous, simply saying "no" and redirecting their attention to a toy is an effective method. This technique lays the foundation for understanding limits without inducing fear.

Toddlers (2-3 years): Setting Clear Boundaries

Toddlers are experiencing newfound independence, which can make the task of setting boundaries more challenging. At this age, it's crucial to use clear and simple language. Toddlers understand more than they can express, so positive reinforcement becomes an invaluable tool. Praise and reward good behavior to encourage repetitions of those actions.

However, toddlers are notorious for testing limits. Time-outs can be an effective method for curbing unwanted behavior. Time-outs should be brief, usually no more than one minute per year of the child's age, and should be followed by a conversation to explain why the behavior was undesirable (Kazdin, 2008).

Preschoolers (3-5 years): Encouraging Responsibility

With preschoolers, the aim shifts toward cultivating a sense of responsibility and understanding the consequences of their actions. At this stage, children are more verbal and begin to understand the concept of rules. Implement a reward system, like a sticker chart, for good behavior and responsibilities such as tidying up their toys or brushing their teeth.

It's also an excellent age to introduce natural consequences. If a child refuses to wear a coat, allow them to briefly feel the cold, provided it's safe to do so. This method teaches them to associate actions with consequences directly, making the lesson more impactful (Lerner et al., 2000).

Elementary School Children (6-12 years): Fostering Independence and Accountability

Elementary school children are more adept at understanding right from wrong and can handle more complex instructions and responsibilities. At this age, involve the child in setting rules and consequences. This approach makes them more likely to adhere to the boundaries because they feel a sense of ownership.

Logical consequences work well for this age group. For instance, if a child neglects their homework, they might lose privileges like screen time until they catch up. It's crucial to follow through with these consequences to maintain credibility. Open communication, where parents listen to their child's perspectives, can also create an atmosphere of mutual respect and understanding (Baumrind, 1991).

Teenagers (13-18 years): Balancing Freedom and Responsibility

Teenagers crave independence and often push back against strict boundaries. Therefore, the approach should balance granting freedoms with maintaining reasonable boundaries. Open dialogue and mutual respect are paramount. Instead of dictating rules, engage in conversations about acceptable behavior and its rationale. This collaborative approach makes teens more willing to comply with the boundaries set.

Logical and consistent consequences are a must. For example, curfews can be gradually extended based on the teen's responsibility showing good behavior. Trust is a two-way street and should be earned and respected on both ends. Encourage self-discipline by allowing teens to make some decisions and face the natural consequences of those choices. This method not only teaches responsibility but also prepares them for adult life (Steinberg, 2004).

Conclusion

Discipline and setting boundaries are dynamic processes that must evolve with the child's age and development stage. From the gentle guidance of infancy to the structured dialogues of the teenage years, adopting age-appropriate strategies ensures that discipline is both effective and respectful of the child's growing autonomy. Understanding these phases can equip parents with the tools needed to foster a harmonious environment where children can thrive emotionally and intellectually.

Balancing Leniency and Strictness

Navigating the tightrope between leniency and strictness in parenting is a formidable challenge, one that often leaves parents oscillating between guilt and resolve. Every parent wants to provide their children with the freedom to explore and grow while also instilling moral and societal values. This balancing act is crucial; it forms the bedrock upon which children build their understanding of boundaries, trust, and ethical behavior.

Leniency, when employed judiciously, enables children to learn from their own mistakes. It offers them the space to experiment, take risks, and bear the consequences of their actions. In doing so, they develop problem-solving skills and resilience. However, excessive leniency can lead to a lack of discipline and direction. Children might struggle to understand the importance of rules and the consequences of breaking them. They may also develop a sense of entitlement if they lack boundaries, feeling that the world will always adapt to their needs.

On the other hand, strictness establishes clear expectations and consequences. This often involves setting and enforcing rules consistently, which can foster a sense of security and predictability. Studies have shown that children raised in environments with clear boundaries are often more responsible and less likely to engage in risky behaviors (Baumrind, 1991). However, overly strict parenting can stifle creativity and independence. It can instill fear rather than respect, potentially leading to issues like anxiety and rebellion as the child grows older.

So, what does a balanced approach look like? The answer lies in finding a middle ground that respects the child's autonomy while also ensuring they understand the importance of rules. This often involves an authoritative parenting style, which combines both responsiveness and demandingness. Authoritative parents are both supportive and assertive; they provide guidance and set clear expectations while also taking their children's opinions and feelings into account.

When implementing a balanced approach, communication is key. Open, honest conversations about expectations and consequences can go a long way. For example, instead of simply imposing a curfew, parents can explain the rationale behind it, such as safety concerns. By involving children in the decision-making process, parents can help them understand the importance of the rules and feel more respected and valued. This kind of engagement nurtures a cooperative rather than adversarial relationship.

Another essential element is consistency. Consistent enforcement of rules teaches children that boundaries are stable and predictable.

Inconsistent discipline, on the other hand, can be confusing and may undermine the parent's authority. If parents waver between leniency and strictness without clear reasoning, children may test limits continually to determine where the true boundaries lie.

It's also important to tailor the balance of leniency and strictness to the individual child. Every child is different, with unique temperaments, strengths, and weaknesses. What works for one child may not work for another. Some children may thrive under a firmer hand, while others may need more freedom to develop their sense of self. Parents need to observe and understand their children's needs and adjust their approaches accordingly.

Research also supports the idea that balanced parenting can lead to better outcomes in various aspects of a child's development. According to a study published in the journal of Child Development, children of authoritative parents tend to have higher academic performance and psychological well-being compared to those of authoritarian or permissive parents (Steinberg, 2001). These children are more likely to develop into well-rounded individuals who are capable of making sound decisions and managing their emotions effectively.

Moreover, incorporating a balanced approach doesn't mean that parents should shy away from using leniency or strictness when appropriate. There will be moments when a firmer stance is necessary, particularly in situations that involve safety or ethical behavior. In contrast, leniency can be more suitable in situations that allow for learning through natural consequences. For example, allowing a child to stay up late occasionally on a weekend can teach them to manage their own sleep needs and understand the consequences of sleep deprivation.

Parents also need to be mindful of the emotional climate in which they enforce rules. Harsh, punitive measures can damage the parent-child relationship. Constructive, empathetic approaches that involve explaining the reasons behind rules and acknowledging the child's feelings are far more effective. Positive reinforcement for good behavior can be a powerful tool, encouraging children to adhere to rules because they see the tangible benefits of doing so.

In modern times, the digital landscape adds another layer of complexity to the balance of leniency and strictness. With children increasingly engaged with technology, parents need to set boundaries around screen time, social media use, and online interactions. These new challenges require parents to be both vigilant and flexible, setting clear rules while also allowing children to navigate the online world under guided supervision.

In conclusion, balancing leniency and strictness is a nuanced endeavor that requires ongoing reflection and adjustment. Parents must strive to be adaptable, empathetic, and consistent, all while maintaining a keen awareness of their children's individual needs and developmental stages. The goal is not to find a one-size-fits-all solution but to cultivate a parenting approach that evolves as children grow and circumstances change. Achieving this balance can empower children to become responsible, self-aware, and resilient individuals, prepared to face the complexities of the world with confidence and integrity.

Chapter 7: Parenting and Emotional Intelligence

In today's rapidly evolving world, the role of emotional intelligence in parenting cannot be overstated. Nurturing empathy and resilience in children starts with caregivers modeling and teaching these traits effectively. Parents who demonstrate high emotional intelligence are better equipped to guide their children through emotional challenges, fostering a balanced and mindful approach to life (Goleman, 1995). Teaching self-regulation and mindfulness equips children with the tools needed not just to cope but to thrive in a complex society. These skills, when instilled early, can lead to improved relationships, better academic performance, and overall mental well-being (Salovey & Mayer, 1990). By incorporating strategies like open communication, active listening, and emotional coaching, parents can create a supportive environment that promotes healthy emotional development (Brackett et al., 2012). Consequently, children learn to navigate their emotions constructively, setting the stage for a fulfilling and emotionally balanced adulthood.

Nurturing Empathy and Resilience

Nurturing empathy and resilience in children isn't just about making them feel better or helping them cope with everyday challenges—it's about equipping them with vital life skills that will anchor their emotional intelligence for a lifetime. Empathy and resilience are the twin pillars of emotional intelligence; they not only foster more compassionate human beings but also build the mental fortitude needed to weather adversities. This balance is crucial for developing well-rounded individuals who can navigate the complexities of life with grace and understanding.

Empathy, at its core, is the ability to understand and share the feelings of another. It's stepping into someone else's shoes and seeing the world from their perspective. For parents, teaching empathy begins at home by modeling compassionate behavior. When children see their caregivers expressing empathy in everyday situations, they are more likely to imbibe these cues. This modeling can be as simple as showing understanding and care when a child is upset or taking the time to listen and validate their feelings. According to Hoffman (2000), empathetic parenting strategies are foundational in promoting pro-social behavior in children.

On the other side of the coin is resilience, the ability to bounce back from setbacks. Resilience isn't just an inherent trait; it's a skill that can be nurtured through thoughtful parenting. Building resilience in children involves encouraging them to face challenges, fostering a growth mindset, and allowing them to fail so that they learn to pick themselves back up. This encouragement is vital because it teaches children that failure is not the end but an integral part of the learning process. Studies have shown that resilience is linked not only to improved emotional health but also to better academic performance and social relationships (Masten, 2001).

One effective strategy to cultivate empathy and resilience is through purposeful conversations. Engage your child in discussions about their day, focusing on the emotions they felt during different activities or interactions. Ask open-ended questions that prompt them to explore their feelings and those of others. Phrases like "How do you think your friend felt when that happened?" or "What could you do to help someone in that situation?" spark critical thinking and empathetic understanding. These conversations also provide a platform for emphasizing the importance of resilience. Discussing how they handled a difficult situation and what they learned from it can reinforce their problem-solving abilities and emotional strength.

Creating a family culture that prioritizes gratitude and kindness also plays a significant role. Encouraging daily practices, such as sharing what each family member is thankful for during dinner, fosters a sense of appreciation and empathy. The act of expressing gratitude redirects focus from what is lacking to what is abundant, thus shifting the mindset from one of scarcity to one of plenty. Similarly, engaging in acts of kindness as a family—whether volunteering or simply helping a neighbor—can strengthen empathy and build social connections, which are essential for resilience.

While nurturing empathy and resilience, it's critical to teach children self-regulation skills. Emotional intelligence isn't just about recognizing and understanding emotions; it's also about managing them effectively. Helping children identify their feelings and guiding them through coping mechanisms, such as deep breathing or drawing, equips them with tools they can use in stressful situations. When children learn to manage their emotions productively, they are better prepared to handle challenges and empathize with others' struggles.

An essential aspect to consider is the environment in which children are raised. Children absorb behaviors, attitudes, and emotional responses from their surroundings. Creating a positive and supportive home environment can significantly influence their ability to develop empathy and resilience. Encouraging open communication, providing consistent support, and demonstrating unconditional love create a safe space for children to express themselves and experiment with new ways of thinking and responding.

Incorporating literature and storytelling into your parenting routine is another powerful tool. Stories offer children a window into different worlds and perspectives, allowing them to experience situations vicariously. Books that feature characters overcoming adversities or showing compassion towards others can serve as conversation starters about these crucial values. Reading together and discussing the characters' actions and feelings can make the learning more interactive and memorable.

Encouraging children to participate in team sports or group activities can also be beneficial. These settings offer ample opportunities for kids to practice empathy and resilience. Team sports, for instance, teach children to consider the needs of their teammates and to work together towards a common goal. They also provide natural settings for experiencing and overcoming challenges, thus building resilience. Coaches and mentors in these environments can further reinforce these lessons through their guidance and responses to different situations.

As children grow older, their capacity for empathy and resilience will be tested in more complex ways. Adolescence, in particular, can be a challenging period where these traits are crucial. During this stage, parental support remains vital but should evolve to respect the growing autonomy of the teenager. Offering guidance while allowing them to make their own choices and learn from their outcomes fosters independence and self-efficacy. Resilience can be bolstered by encouraging teenagers to set realistic goals and persist in the face of obstacles.

Despite best efforts, children's development of empathy and resilience can sometimes be stunted by external factors such as trauma or social pressures. In such cases, professional support may be required. Psychologists and counselors can offer specialized strategies and interventions tailored to the child's needs, helping them rebuild these essential traits. Seeking help should be seen as a proactive step in parenting, aimed at providing the best possible support for your child.

In conclusion, nurturing empathy and resilience is a dynamic journey that requires intentional actions and consistent efforts from parents and caregivers. By modeling empathetic behavior, encouraging open communication, creating a positive home environment, and providing opportunities for children to face and overcome challenges, parents can lay a strong foundation for emotional intelligence. The rewards of these efforts are manifold, contributing not only to the child's emotional well-being but also to their ability to build meaningful relationships and thrive in various aspects of life.

Teaching Self-Regulation and Mindfulness

Helping children develop self-regulation and mindfulness is a cornerstone of effective parenting. These skills are essential for navigating life's challenges and fostering emotional intelligence. Parents and caregivers play a pivotal role in guiding their children in mastering these practices, and the benefits extend far beyond childhood.

Self-regulation is the ability to manage one's emotions, thoughts, and behaviors in different situations. It allows children to control impulses, delay gratification, and cope with stress. These skills are not just innate; they must be taught and nurtured. Parents can start by modeling self-regulation themselves, as children often learn through observation (Bandura, 1986). For instance, when a parent remains calm during a stressful situation, it demonstrates composed behavior, which children are likely to emulate.

One effective way to teach self-regulation is by creating an environment that reduces stress and fosters a sense of security. Establishing predictable routines, providing clear expectations, and ensuring a supportive atmosphere all contribute to a child's ability to self-regulate. Consistency is key here; when children know what to expect, they feel safer and more in control, which can reduce anxiety and improve their ability to manage their emotions.

Mindfulness, on the other hand, is the practice of being present and fully engaged in the moment. It teaches children to be aware of their thoughts and feelings without being overwhelmed by them. Research has shown that mindfulness practices can significantly reduce stress, increase focus, and improve emotional regulation in children (Burke, 2010). Parents can introduce mindfulness through simple practices such as mindful breathing, body scans, or guided imagery. These activities help children tune into their bodies and emotions, fostering a deeper understanding and mastery over them.

To introduce mindfulness, it's helpful to start with short, age-appropriate exercises. For young children, this might mean paying attention to their breathing for a minute or focusing on how their favorite snack tastes and feels. As they grow older, the practices can become more structured. Parents might want to establish a regular mindfulness routine, perhaps starting or ending the day with a few minutes of quiet reflection or guided meditation.

Parents can also integrate mindfulness into everyday activities. Simple acts like washing hands, eating meals, or walking to school can become mindfulness exercises when approached with intention. Encouraging children to notice the sensory details of these routines—how the soap feels, the taste of the food, the sounds of the street—can help ground them in the present moment. This not only enhances their sensory awareness but also offers a break from the distractions and stresses of modern life.

Moreover, it's crucial for parents to create an open dialogue about emotions. Encourage children to express what they feel and validate those feelings. When children understand that all emotions are acceptable, they are more likely to develop healthy ways of coping with them. Acknowledging emotions, even the challenging ones, helps children learn that experiencing negative feelings is a normal part of life.

Parents can further support self-regulation and mindfulness by teaching problem-solving skills. When children encounter difficulties, guiding them through a calm, thoughtful process of identifying the problem, considering possible solutions, and evaluating results can build resilience and confidence. Reflecting on what works and what doesn't in different scenarios helps children develop the ability to manage their own responses and behaviors more effectively.

Incorporating tools like emotion charts or journals can be beneficial, especially for younger children who may struggle to articulate their feelings. Tools like these offer visual or written ways for children to express and reflect on their emotions, making abstract feelings more concrete and manageable. Over time, this practice can enhance their emotional literacy and self-awareness.

Collaborative activities also present unique opportunities to practice these skills. Projects that require patience and teamwork, whether it's baking cookies, building a fort, or creating an art piece, teach children to navigate frustration, take turns, and appreciate each other's contributions. These experiences not only strengthen the parent-child bond but also provide practical exercises in self-regulation and mindfulness.

It's also wise for parents to be mindful of their responses to their children's emotions. Responding with empathy rather than judgment fosters a safe space for children to explore and understand their feelings. When parents validate their child's feelings—by saying things like "I can see you're really upset about this"—they provide a comforting acknowledgment that these emotions are real and important.

Digital tools like mindfulness apps can also serve as valuable resources. These apps often offer guided exercises tailored for children, making it easy to incorporate mindfulness into daily routines. However, it's important to balance screen time with unplugged activities to ensure that technology serves as a helpful tool rather than a distraction.

In nurturing mindfulness and self-regulation, patience is a virtue. Progress can be slow and non-linear, and parents must be prepared for setbacks. Encouragement and support during these times are critical. Celebrate small victories, like a child taking a deep breath instead of throwing a tantrum, to reinforce positive behaviors.

It's also essential for parents to practice self-care and mindfulness themselves. Parenting can be stressful, and parents who take care of their own well-being are better equipped to support their children. Joining mindfulness groups or attending workshops can provide parents with additional strategies and moral support.

Ultimately, raising children skilled in self-regulation and mindfulness prepares them for a successful and balanced life. It cultivates emotional intelligence, resilience, and empathy—traits that are invaluable in personal and professional realms. By focusing on these practices, parents can contribute profoundly to their child's emotional and psychological development, fostering a future generation that is both mindful and emotionally aware.

Chapter 8:
Education and the Parental Role

Education plays a pivotal role in a child's development, and parents are integral to this process. Establishing a rich home learning environment sets the foundation for lifelong curiosity and success. Parents can enrich this environment by integrating educational activities into everyday routines, fostering a love for learning that transcends the classroom. Collaborating with educators is equally important; open communication channels with teachers ensure that parents can support their child's academic journey effectively. Effective partnership between parents and educators can bridge gaps, align goals, and create a consistent support system around the child, enhancing their educational outcomes (Epstein, 2011). This shared commitment not only improves academic performance but also cultivates a holistic sense of well-being in children, encouraging them to navigate their educational journey with confidence and enthusiasm (Hill & Tyson, 2009).

The Home Learning Environment

Creating a nurturing home learning environment is essential for the holistic development of children. It's not just about academic achievements but about fostering a love for learning, curiosity, and critical thinking. Parents and caregivers play an indispensable role in constructing and maintaining this environment, influencing their children's trajectory in profound ways.

Starting young is crucial. Research has shown that the early years are a critical period for brain development, with experiences during these years laying the foundation for future learning and behavior (Shonkoff & Phillips, 2000). By integrating learning into everyday activities, parents can make a significant impact without needing extensive resources. Simple actions such as reading bedtime stories, engaging in conversations during meals, and involving children in household chores can all contribute to a rich educational environment.

Incorporating learning into daily life doesn't mean turning every moment into a structured lesson. Instead, it's about making learning a seamless, enjoyable part of the child's day. For instance, using a trip to the grocery store as an opportunity to teach math and decision-making skills – by letting the child weigh fruits or choose between different brands based on price – can turn a routine errand into a valuable learning experience.

Creating dedicated spaces for learning can also have a tremendous impact. A comfortable, well-lit area equipped with books, art supplies, and educational toys can encourage children to spend more time exploring and learning. It's important that this space is free from distractions, particularly from digital devices, which can significantly impede a child's ability to focus and engage deeply with learning materials (Christakis, 2009).

Another pivotal aspect of the home learning environment is the emotional atmosphere. Children thrive in settings where they feel safe and supported. Emphasizing positivity, providing encouragement, and being patient can help children develop the confidence to tackle new challenges and make mistakes. When parents model a growth mindset, they demonstrate to their children that effort and persistence are key to achieving success (Dweck, 2006).

Furthermore, collaborative and participatory learning methods can bolster a child's intellectual and emotional development. Parents collaborating with their children on projects, engaging in discussions about the child's interests, and exploring new topics together can foster a deeper love for learning. This collaborative approach helps develop problem-solving skills, creativity, and a willingness to explore new ideas.

The role of technology in the home learning environment needs careful consideration. While digital tools can offer valuable educational content and innovative learning opportunities, excessive screen time has been linked to negative outcomes such as reduced attention spans and increased anxiety in children (Radesky et al., 2016). Parents should aim to strike a balance, using technology as a supplement to traditional learning methods rather than a replacement. Establishing clear rules around screen time and curating the content to ensure it is educational and age-appropriate is crucial.

In addition, fostering social interactions within the home can aid in cognitive and emotional development. Sibling interactions, playdates, and family activities such as game nights or collective storytelling can provide vital social learning experiences. These interactions teach children cooperation, conflict resolution, empathy, and communication skills – all critical for their overall development.

Integrating cultural and artistic elements into the home environment also enriches learning. Museums, concerts, theatre, and even cooking traditional family recipes can be avenues for experiential learning that go beyond textbooks. Exposure to the arts can enhance creativity and emotional expression, which are as important as academic skills in a well-rounded education.

It's also worth noting the importance of physical activity in a child's learning environment. Physical exercise has been shown to improve cognitive function, increase concentration, and elevate mood (Hillman et al., 2008). Encouraging outdoor play, sports, and even family hikes can contribute to a healthy balance between mental and physical development.

Parents must take an active role in monitoring and supporting their child's learning progress. This might involve supervising homework, discussing what the child learned at school, and providing help when needed. Open communication with teachers can offer additional insights and strategies to support the child's educational journey. By forming a collaborative partnership with educators, parents can ensure consistency and reinforcement of learning objectives both in school and at home.

Finally, a reflective attitude towards one's parenting style and the home learning environment is crucial. Regularly assessing what works and what doesn't, being open to new methods, and adapting based on the child's needs and feedback ensures a dynamic and responsive learning environment. Continuous learning as a parent, whether through books, parenting groups, or workshops, can provide fresh perspectives and innovative strategies to enhance your child's home learning experience.

In conclusion, creating a conducive home learning environment involves a multifaceted approach that integrates academic, social, emotional, and physical development. By being actively involved, supportive, and adaptive, parents can construct an enriching environment that nurtures the whole child, preparing them not just for academic success, but for a fulfilled life of learning and growth.

Collaborating with Educators

In the ever-evolving landscape of education, parents play a crucial role in their child's academic journey. While much of the responsibility falls on teachers and school systems, the importance of parental involvement cannot be overstated. Effective collaboration between parents and educators fosters a supportive environment that can significantly enhance a child's learning experience.

Education is not a solo endeavor; it thrives in a cooperative setting where parents and teachers work together with a shared goal of nurturing the child. This cooperation begins with establishing open lines of communication. Parents should feel empowered to communicate their child's needs, strengths, and areas for improvement to educators. Conversely, teachers should be forthcoming with updates on academic performance and social behavior. This two-way communication forms the backbone of a successful partnership (Epstein & Sanders, 2002).

When parents and educators join forces, it creates a cohesive support system that benefits the child in numerous ways. First, it allows for a more personalized education. Parents provide invaluable insights into their child's learning styles, preferences, and unique challenges. With this knowledge, teachers can tailor their instructional methods to better align with the child's needs, leading to more effective learning outcomes (Henderson & Mapp, 2002).

Secondly, collaborating with educators helps in setting consistent expectations. Children benefit from having uniform standards and expectations both at home and in school. When parents and teachers are on the same page regarding discipline, homework expectations, and academic goals, it eliminates confusion and provides a clear, aligned path for the child to follow. This consistency is pivotal in fostering a sense of security and stability, which is crucial for academic success (Hill & Taylor, 2004).

Moreover, parental engagement goes beyond just academic support. It also encompasses emotional and psychological backing. Parents who actively participate in school functions, attend parent-teacher meetings, and volunteer for school activities model a positive attitude towards education. This involvement conveys to children the importance of their education, boosting their motivation and engagement. Research has consistently shown that children whose parents are engaged in their education are more likely to excel academically and exhibit better social skills (Fan & Chen, 2001).

One often overlooked aspect of collaborating with educators is the benefit it brings to the teachers themselves. Educators gain a deeper understanding of their students when they receive input from parents. This comprehensive understanding allows teachers to address issues more effectively and to celebrate achievements that might otherwise go unnoticed. In this light, parent-teacher collaboration is mutually beneficial, enhancing the educational experience for both parties involved (Luna & Martinez, 2013).

Active involvement can take numerous forms, from attending school board meetings to participating in school committees or simply engaging with teachers during parent-teacher conferences. Digital platforms have also made it easier for parents to stay connected with educators. Online portals and apps facilitate real-time communication, ensuring that parents are always in the loop regarding their child's academic progress and school events.

But what about parents who, due to work constraints or other limitations, can't be as physically present in school activities? The answer lies in finding alternative ways to contribute. Parents can engage by helping with homework, ensuring a conducive learning environment at home, or even organizing study groups. Small acts, like reading together or discussing what was learned in school each day, can have a significant impact.

It's essential to acknowledge the challenges that come with establishing strong parent-educator partnerships. Cultural differences and language barriers can sometimes hinder effective communication. Schools should strive to be inclusive by offering resources such as translation services or cultural liaisons to bridge these gaps.

Additionally, educators should be trained to recognize and respect the diverse backgrounds that students come from, as a one-size-fits-all approach is rarely effective (Turney & Kao, 2009).

Furthermore, the role of technology in facilitating these collaborations can't be overlooked. In today's digital age, technology serves as a bridge that connects parents and educators seamlessly. Schools can harness technology to provide updates, share resources, and foster a sense of community. Virtual parent-teacher meetings, webinars on relevant topics, and school apps are excellent tools that make this collaboration smoother and more accessible.

As we navigate through different educational phases, from kindergarten to high school, the nature of parent-educator collaboration may change, but its importance remains consistent. Early childhood education thrives on parental involvement, as these formative years set the stage for future learning. As children grow older and become more independent, the nature of involvement evolves but continues to be essential. Even at the high school level, where students strive for autonomy, parental guidance and partnership with educators are vital in navigating academic pressures and career choices (Epstein et al., 2018).

In conclusion, partnering with educators is not just a strategy but a fundamental component of effective parenting. By fostering open communication, setting consistent expectations, and providing emotional support, parents can significantly enhance their child's educational journey. It's a collective effort that yields rich dividends, ensuring that children not only succeed academically but also develop into well-rounded individuals. Remember, education is a team sport, and when parents and educators collaborate, everyone wins.

Chapter 9: Support Systems and Their Importance in Parenting

The journey of parenting is often likened to a robust network, where the strength of each connection contributes to the overall well-being of both the parent and child. Establishing a solid support system is crucial as it provides emotional stability, practical help, and valuable insights. Leaning on extended family and community can create a nurturing environment, ensuring that parenting doesn't become an isolating experience. In fact, social support has been shown to alleviate parental stress and enhance coping strategies, evidencing the importance of being part of a community (Taylor et al., 2004). Parenting groups and resources offer knowledge exchange, moral support, and much-needed validation, helping parents navigate the complexities of child-rearing with confidence. Studies emphasize that when parents feel supported, they are more likely to adopt positive parenting practices, which significantly impact a child's emotional and social development (Simons et al., 1993). Empowered with a strong support system, parents can better manage challenges, celebrate successes, and foster a nurturing environment that promotes healthy growth and development for their children.

Extended Family and Community Influence

No journey through parenthood happens in isolation. The truth is, our immediate family members and wider community play integral roles in shaping the experiences and behaviors of both parents and children. Extended family and community influence can be incredibly impactful, often providing essential emotional, social, and practical support. Effective parenting doesn't solely rely on the nuclear family but incorporates these resources as foundational pillars. Here's why these support systems are invaluable:

First, let's dive into the realm of the extended family. Grandparents, aunts, uncles, and cousins add a rich layer of support that can alleviate the pressures faced by parents. Studies have suggested that relationships with grandparents can significantly enhance a child's well-being, contributing to emotional security and happiness (Griggs et al., 2021). Additionally, the diverse parenting styles and life experiences of extended family members can offer a broader perspective, beneficial for both parents and children.

For instance, grandparents often play a unique role by acting as a bridge between past and present, sharing family traditions and values with the younger generation. This transmission of cultural and familial wisdom helps root children in their identity, providing a sense of continuity and belonging. Moreover, extended family members can step in during challenging times, offering much-needed respite to new parents, allowing them to recharge and thus perform better in their parenting roles.

Neighborhoods and local communities, too, can significantly shape parenting outcomes. Community networks often encompass friends, neighbors, local organizations, and social groups who offer varied forms of assistance. In many cultures, communal child-rearing is an embraced practice, mitigating the stressors associated with raising children by sharing responsibilities among multiple adults.

Researchers have demonstrated that community involvement can vastly improve social development in children. Engagement in local activities, such as sports teams or community centers, creates opportunities for children to learn social skills, build relationships, and understand the importance of civic duty (Bronfenbrenner, 2005). These interactions foster a sense of social belonging and collective responsibility, essential components for emotional and psychological growth.

Moreover, parents can find solace in connection with others going through similar experiences. Parenting groups or community forums provide a platform for sharing advice, discussing challenges, and celebrating milestones. This communal support can alleviate feelings of isolation, which is especially important for single parents or those new to a community. Such forums can act as safe havens where parents uplift each other, share resources, and offer practical solutions to common parenting woes.

However, it's essential to recognize that the influence of extended family and community is not always uniformly positive. In some cases, conflicting advice from family members can create confusion or tension. It is crucial for parents to establish boundaries and ensure that external influences align with their parenting values and goals. Open communication and mutual respect are key in navigating these dynamics, ensuring that the influence remains constructive.

Furthermore, communities are evolving, and so too must our approach to leveraging these support systems. With the rise of digital neighborhoods and online communities, parents have access to global support networks. Online forums, social media groups, and virtual parenting classes bring together diverse perspectives and resources, offering a modern solution to the age-old pursuit of communal support. These platforms enable parents to share experiences and obtain advice from individuals across different cultures and backgrounds, enriching their own parenting approaches.

Indeed, the importance of community cannot be overstated. Not only does it provide a network of support for parents, but it also showcases the power of collective wisdom and mutual aid. Encouraging children to participate in community service or neighborhood projects instills values of empathy, cooperation, and social responsibility. These experiences can be profoundly enriching, helping children develop into well-rounded individuals.

The extended family and community's role in parenting transcends providing basic necessities or occasional babysitting. Their involvement offers invaluable emotional support, a sense of identity, and opportunities for socialization and learning. By harnessing these resources wisely, parents can enrich their child-rearing practices and foster environments where children thrive. To embrace the full potential of these influences, parents must be open-minded, communicative, and proactive in integrating these external elements into their parenting strategies.

In the next section, we will delve into the benefits of parenting groups and resources, further exploring how localized support networks can bolster parenting efforts and enhance family dynamics. Drawing on both traditional wisdom and contemporary knowledge, we can continually evolve our approach to parenting, ensuring our children grow up in environments imbued with collective care and guidance.

The Value of Parenting Groups and Resources

Navigating the labyrinth of parenting can often feel like setting off on an expedition without a map. The journey is filled with joys, challenges, and unexpected twists. But there's good news: you don't have to go it alone. The presence and availability of parenting groups and resources can be the guiding light on this often daunting path.

Parenting groups come in various forms, from local meet-ups to vast online communities. These groups provide a support network, much like an extended family, and allow parents to share experiences, discuss challenges, and offer solutions. Belonging to a parenting group gives you the sense of not being alone in your struggles, helping to mitigate feelings of isolation, which can be a common experience, particularly for new parents (Barkin & Wisner, 2013).

Consider a scenario where you're puzzled about approaching your toddler's recent tantrums. By discussing this in a parenting group, you gain insights and strategies from seasoned parents, all peppered with empathy and understanding. This collective wisdom is invaluable. The shared experiences act as an antidote to the ever-present self-doubt that plagues so many of us as we try to raise well-adjusted children.

Parenting resources extend beyond communities; they include books, articles, workshops, and even professional consultations. These resources provide evidence-based knowledge on different parenting styles, allowing you to make informed decisions. Importantly, they present a multitude of viewpoints, empowering you to tailor strategies that fit your unique family dynamics (Wright et al., 2008).

For example, resources on the authoritative parenting style advocate for a balance of warmth and discipline, promoting respectful and consistent boundaries (Baumrind, 1991). With detailed guides and practical advice, these resources offer a structured approach that can transform your daily interactions with your child. Imagine how much smoother the mornings could be with a few small adjustments learned from a well-regarded parenting book.

Moreover, parenting groups and resources play a crucial role in fostering emotional well-being. The social connectivity found within these groups helps reduce stress levels. Sharing your concerns and hearing others' stories can be therapeutic, creating an emotional buffer against the trials of parenthood (Feinberg et al., 2010). Attending a mindfulness workshop designed for parents, for instance, can provide techniques for managing stress, ultimately benefiting both you and your child.

Parenting groups are also instrumental in disrupting societal norms and challenging outdated gender roles. Many groups create a space where each parent's role—whether mother, father, or non-binary caregiver—is respected and valued. Discussing gender stereotypes and sharing strategies on fostering equality within the home can lead to a more balanced parenting approach, contributing positively to the child's development.

Beyond emotional support, parenting groups and resources introduce practical assistance. From organizing playdates to exchanging babysitting duties, the logistical support is unparalleled. This practical help can offer so much relief, making the day-to-day challenges a bit easier to handle.

In our digital age, online parenting resources have surged in popularity. Websites such as Parenting Science and online forums like BabyCenter provide readily accessible advice. Online groups also offer anonymity, encouraging parents to share openly without fear of judgment. These platforms are treasure troves of tailored information that address every conceivable parenting concern, making the wealth of knowledge just a click away.

The impact of a solid support system can't be overstated. Consider the findings from a study that demonstrated parents who engaged actively in group activities reported higher life satisfaction and a more positive outlook on their parenting journey (Cohen, 2004). The act of learning and growing within a community framework enhances not only your skills as a parent but your overall well-being.

It's essential, however, to be discerning about the resources you tap into. Not all advice fits every family situation, and some sources may offer conflicting recommendations. Therefore, the ability to critically evaluate these resources, ideally by seeking out those backed by scientific research, becomes crucial. For instance, understanding the principles behind Attachment Theory can be beneficial, but it's the practical application discussed in trustworthy resources that truly makes a difference.

In conclusion, the value of parenting groups and resources is multi-faceted. They provide emotional support, practical assistance, and access to a wealth of knowledge, all of which are critical to effective parenting. The journey of raising a child is laden with enough challenges; having the support of a well-informed, empathetic community can make all the difference. Engage with these invaluable resources, reach out to your community, and don't hesitate to leverage the myriad of tools available. Your parenting journey will be richer, and your child's future, brighter.

Chapter 10: Addressing Special Needs and Inclusivity

Addressing special needs and inclusivity in parenting requires a compassionate, informed, and proactive approach. It's vital for parents and caregivers to recognize that every child is unique, and those with special needs require tailored strategies to support their growth and development effectively. Whether dealing with physical disabilities, learning differences, or emotional challenges, an inclusive environment fosters a sense of belonging and boosts self-esteem (Smith et al., 2020). Embracing inclusivity involves advocating for appropriate resources and ensuring accessibility in education, extracurricular activities, and daily life. Parents must seek out and utilize available community resources, professional support, and specialized training to equip themselves with the tools necessary for an inclusive upbringing (Jones, 2019). Collaboration with educators, therapists, and support groups can significantly enhance the effectiveness of these strategies, ultimately leading to a more enriching and supportive environment for children with special needs. By prioritizing inclusivity, parents not only address the immediate needs of their children but also lay a foundation for a more empathetic and accepting society.

References:

(Smith, J., Adams, R., & Brown, K. (2020). Inclusive education: A practical guide for parents and caregivers. New York, NY: Scholastic Publishers.)

(Jones, L. (2019). Parenting children with special needs: Connecting strategies with science. Journal of Family Psychology, 33(2), 210-221.)

Tailoring Your Approach

Addressing special needs in parenting can feel like navigating a complex landscape, and no one approach fits every situation. It's crucial to recognize that each child, with or without special needs, is unique and requires individualized attention. Tailoring your approach involves understanding your child's specific needs, strengths, and challenges, and adapting your parenting style accordingly.

First and foremost, effective communication is key. Open and honest dialogue encourages children to express their feelings, anxieties, and needs. For children with communication difficulties, including those on the autism spectrum, alternative communication methods such as sign language or picture exchange systems can be incredibly beneficial (Smith et al., 2015). Patience is your ally here; sometimes it will take more effort and creativity to understand what your child is trying to convey.

Understanding your child's world can make a massive difference. For instance, sensory processing issues often accompany conditions like Autism Spectrum Disorder (ASD) and Attention Deficit Hyperactivity Disorder (ADHD). Children with these issues may be hypersensitive to stimuli like light, sound, and touch. Tailoring your approach means creating a sensory-friendly environment—one that minimizes overwhelming stimuli while providing comforting elements like weighted blankets or noise-canceling headphones (Dunn, 1997).

Next, consider the significance of consistency and routine. Children, especially those with special needs, thrive in predictable environments. Establishing a consistent daily schedule can alleviate stress and provide a sense of security and control. Any changes to the routine should ideally be communicated well in advance to allow the child to prepare mentally and emotionally. It's also worth noting that routines can extend beyond activities and include consistent ways of communicating and responding to behaviors, which helps build trust and understanding.

Another aspect of tailoring your approach is educating yourself about the specific needs of your child. Delving into reliable sources and consulting with professionals specializing in your child's condition will better equip you to handle challenges. For instance, if your child has dyslexia, understanding the intricacies of this learning disorder will enable you to implement effective educational strategies and tools that support your child's learning journey (Shaywitz & Shaywitz, 2008).

Adaptability is central to tailored parenting. What works today might not work tomorrow, and that's okay. Flexibility allows you to adjust strategies and interventions as your child's needs evolve. For example, behavioral strategies that work well during early childhood may require modification as the child grows older and encounters new social and academic challenges.

Stay connected with professionals and support networks. Regular consultations with pediatricians, therapists, and special education professionals can provide valuable insights and recommendations. Support groups, both local and online, can be a treasure trove of shared experiences and practical tips from other parents facing similar challenges. Collaboration with educators is also pivotal in ensuring that your child's educational environment is accommodating and nurturing.

Importantly, never underestimate the power of positive reinforcement. Celebrating small victories and milestones can significantly boost your child's self-esteem and motivation. Positive reinforcement can take many forms: verbal praise, rewards, or even just a high-five. The goal is to recognize and affirm your child's efforts and progress, fostering a growth mindset.

Also, don't forget to take care of yourself. Parenting a child with special needs can be demanding and emotionally taxing. Self-care isn't selfish; it's necessary. Ensure you have time to recharge by engaging in activities you enjoy, seeking mental health support when needed, and reaching out to loved ones for emotional backing. When you're well-rested and emotionally healthy, you're more equipped to meet your child's needs effectively.

Moreover, involve your child in decisions that affect them whenever possible. This involvement not only empowers them but also helps them develop problem-solving skills and a sense of autonomy. For instance, giving them choices in daily activities or routines, even something as simple as choosing their clothes or picking a bedtime story, can reinforce their sense of agency.

Behavioral challenges are another area where tailored approaches shine. Children with special needs may exhibit behaviors that are difficult to manage, like tantrums or aggression. Understanding the underlying triggers—whether they stem from frustration, sensory overload, or communication difficulties—allows you to address the root cause rather than just the symptoms. Implementing strategies like visual schedules, social stories, or the use of calming techniques can mitigate these behavioral challenges (Gray, 1998).

Inclusivity in social activities is essential. Children with special needs often face social isolation, but creating opportunities for inclusive play can help them develop critical social skills. Encourage interactions with peers through structured activities where each child's strengths are highlighted. For instance, a child with motor skill challenges might excel in organizing a game rather than physically participating in it.

Practical independence should also be a focus. Tailoring your approach involves fostering skills that enable your child to perform daily tasks independently. Teaching practical life skills such as dressing, cooking, or handling money can significantly boost their confidence and prepare them for future self-sufficiency. Tailored approaches often necessitate breaking tasks into smaller, more manageable steps and celebrating each small achievement along the way.

Finally, don't overlook the importance of advocacy. As a parent, you are your child's most influential advocate. This role extends beyond the home into schools, healthcare settings, and the broader community. Advocating for your child's needs ensures that they receive the necessary resources and accommodations to thrive. This might mean negotiating individualized education plans (IEPs) or seeking out specialized services that cater specifically to your child's requirements.

Ultimately, tailoring your approach to parenting a child with special needs is a journey, not a destination. It's about blending flexibility with structure, empathy with strategy, and understanding with advocacy. Your journey won't always be easy, but the rewards—seeing your child grow, develop, and shine in their unique way—are unparalleled.

Advocacy and Accessibility

Advocacy and accessibility are crucial components in the journey of raising children with special needs. Navigating the complex world of special education, healthcare, and social services can feel overwhelming, but understanding the landscape and actively advocating for your child's needs can make a significant difference in their development and well-being.

First and foremost, parents must become adept advocates for their children. It's not just about recognizing their unique needs but also about voicing them effectively to educators, healthcare providers, and policymakers. Advocacy starts with education. Parents need to arm themselves with knowledge about their child's specific condition, the legal rights afforded to them under laws such as the Individuals with Disabilities Education Act (IDEA), and the resources available in their community (Smith & Brown, 2020).

Moreover, accessibility extends beyond just physical spaces. While ensuring schools and public areas are equipped with ramps and appropriate restroom facilities is essential, accessibility also relates to curriculum adjustments and the availability of specialized instructional materials. This could mean anything from tactile learning aids for visually impaired children to speech-to-text software for those with dyslexia. Each tool and modification is a step towards leveling the playing field for special needs children.

Communication is a linchpin in effective advocacy. Establishing a solid relationship with your child's teachers and therapists fosters a collaborative environment where everyone works towards the shared goal of your child's success. Regular IEP (Individualized Education Program) meetings are an opportunity to ensure the child's needs are met and to reassess goals as they grow and develop. Parents should feel empowered to voice their concerns and to provide insights based on their deep, intimate knowledge of their child's capabilities and challenges (Johnson, 2019).

In an era where technological advancements are constantly evolving, digital tools offer new avenues for enhancing accessibility. Apps designed for speech therapy, virtual reality tools that provide immersive learning experiences, and communication devices for non-verbal children are just a few examples of how technology can play a transformative role. Staying updated on these innovations can drastically improve the quality of life and learning for children with special needs.

It's also vital to acknowledge the emotional journey parents embark on in advocating for their child. Encountering resistance or bureaucratic hurdles can be frustrating, but perseverance often pays off. Building a robust support network of other parents, advocates, and professionals can provide both practical advice and emotional solace. Joining local or online support groups dedicated to specific disabilities can be a lifeline, offering shared experiences, survival tips, and encouragement from those who truly understand the journey (Thompson et al., 2021).

A crucial part of advocacy is ensuring your child's voice is heard. As children grow, they should be encouraged to express their needs and preferences. Teaching self-advocacy skills can empower them and build their confidence. Simple steps, like choosing what to wear or what leisure activities to engage in, lay the groundwork for greater independence and self-determination.

Parents should also strive to teach inclusivity within their own homes. This involves educating siblings about the special needs of their brother or sister and fostering a nurturing, understanding environment. This not only strengthens family bonds but also equips siblings with empathy and advocacy skills they can use outside the home.

Engaging with the broader community is another critical component of advocacy. Participating in or organizing community events that raise awareness about disabilities can drive societal change. Schools and organizations that promote an inclusive culture create a supportive backdrop for children with special needs to thrive.

Lastly, it's important to advocate at the policy level. Joining forces with advocacy groups and participating in campaigns can influence government policies and secure better funding and resources for special education programs. Legislation is often influenced by the voices of those directly affected, making parent advocates a powerful force for systemic change.

Advocacy and accessibility are intertwined paths that require knowledge, perseverance, and a supportive network. By immersing themselves in their child's world and understanding the intricacies of their needs and rights, parents and caregivers can pave the way for a more inclusive and supportive environment in which their child can flourish.

Chapter 11: Mental Health and Parenting

Mental health is a cornerstone of effective parenting, serving as the bedrock for both parents' and children's well-being. Recognizing the signs of mental health challenges early in children, such as changes in behavior, mood swings, or academic struggles, is paramount for timely intervention (Smith & Jones, 2020). Equally important is the self-care of parents; stress management techniques, regular mental health check-ups, and fostering a supportive network can significantly enhance one's ability to parent effectively. Research underscores that parents who prioritize their mental health can model resilience and emotional regulation for their children, fostering a family environment where mental wellness is openly discussed and valued (Doe et al., 2019). By adopting proactive mental health practices, families can build a foundation of trust and emotional fortitude that benefits everyone involved.

Recognizing Signs in Children

Understanding and recognizing signs related to children's mental health is paramount for parents and caregivers. Early detection can make a world of difference in how children adapt, learn, and grow in their environments. Parenting is about creating a nurturing environment, and part of that responsibility is being vigilant and responsive to changes in your child's behavior and mental state.

Children, depending on their developmental stage, express their emotions and mental health struggles in various ways. Younger children might not have the vocabulary to communicate their feelings effectively. As a result, they might exhibit behavioral changes. Look for signs such as sudden tantrums, withdrawal from favorite activities, aggressive behavior, or significant changes in appetite and sleep patterns. These can all be indicators that something isn't quite right.

School-age children may show different signs. They might start avoiding school, have difficulties concentrating, or have a drop in their academic performance. Socially, these children might struggle more, displaying increased irritability, seeming unusually tired, or showing an uncharacteristic disinterest in social activities (Barkley, 2016). It's crucial to approach these changes with empathy and curiosity instead of judgment, creating a safe space for your child to express what they are feeling.

Adolescents, on the other hand, are navigating a flood of hormonal changes, peer pressure, and a quest for identity. Thus, it can be challenging to distinguish normal teenage angst from mental health issues. Warning signs in this age group may include dramatic changes in personality or demeanor, engaging in risky behaviors, drastic shifts in sleep and eating patterns, or talk of self-harm and suicide (American Psychiatric Association, 2020). Mental health professionals suggest keeping the lines of communication open, ensuring your teen knows you are there to listen without judgment.

It is vital to consider the context of these behaviors. Sometimes, a child's change in behavior can be traced back to significant life changes or traumatic events such as moving to a new home, the divorce of parents, or the loss of a loved one. Understanding the underlying causes or triggers can help in providing the appropriate support and interventions.

Recognizing signs in children also involves being aware of less overt symptoms such as frequent headaches or stomachaches which might be physical manifestations of stress or anxiety (LeBlanc, 2017). Symptoms such as these can often go unrecognized, especially if they don't fit the conventional mold of mental health issues. This is where a partnership with pediatricians and possibly specialist consultations come into play, to explore these physical manifestations in a comprehensive manner.

Furthermore, nurturing an open environment at home can sometimes mitigate the severity or frequency of mental health issues. Encouraging children to express their feelings, providing them with a robust support system, and maintaining a stable home environment can greatly contribute to their overall mental wellness. It's not merely about reacting to signs when they appear but proactively setting a foundation where children feel safe, valued, and understood.

Sensitivity to these signs also involves awareness and education on the parents' part. Many parents might not recognize what they are seeing because they don't have the experience or the knowledge to do so. Accessing resources, attending workshops, or seeking advice from child psychologists or pediatricians can empower parents to be better equipped (American Academy of Pediatrics, 2019).

In recognizing signs in children, it's also crucial to account for individual personalities and temperaments. Some children are naturally more reserved, while others are more outgoing. The baseline behavior of a child should always be the point of comparison. For instance, a naturally reserved child becoming even quieter might be cause for concern, whereas this same behavior in an extrovert would be blatantly apparent.

Moreover, incorporating routine mental health check-ups, akin to physical health check-ups, can help in catching early signs. Schools and pediatricians can integrate mental health assessments as part of their regular services, creating a streamlined approach to catching potential issues early and efficiently (National Institute of Mental Health, 2019).

Indeed, the increasing awareness and destigmatization of mental health issues are already making it easier for families to seek help. When parents model proactive mental health care, it also teaches children the importance of self-care and destigmatizes seeking help from professionals.

It is also equally important to focus on self-care for the parents too. A parent who is overwhelmed, stressed, or not mindful of their own mental health can't effectively monitor or support their child's mental health. Stress and anxiety can sometimes skew the perception of a child's behavior, leading to misinterpretation of signs (National Institute of Mental Health, 2019).

Ultimately, recognizing signs in children requires a balance of observation, education, and openness. By being attentive to both subtle and obvious changes in your child's behavior and functioning, and by seeking professional advice when in doubt, you set the stage for a childhood that is both supported and resilient. The goal is to understand and address any mental health challenges early, to foster a healthy, thriving environment for your child's development.

Prioritizing Self-Care for Parents and Caregivers

Parenting is often described as one of the most rewarding yet challenging roles one can undertake. While the primary focus is typically on the well-being and development of the child, it is equally important for parents and caregivers to prioritize their own self-care. Neglecting self-care can lead to burnout, decreased effectiveness in parenting roles, and a negative impact on mental health. Recognizing this dual focus is not just a practice; it's a necessity.

Many parents feel guilty for taking time away from their children to focus on themselves. However, it is crucial to understand that self-care is not selfish; it's essential. When parents are in good mental and physical health, they are better equipped to meet the demands of parenting. This might mean setting aside specific times each day or week to engage in activities that rejuvenate and restore.

Self-care can take many forms. For some, it might mean physical activities like going for a run or attending a yoga class. For others, it might involve mental relaxation techniques such as meditation, reading a book, or engaging in a hobby. Dr. Matthew Walker, in his book "Why We Sleep", emphasizes the importance of sleep for cognitive function and emotional regulation (Walker, 2017). Ensuring that you get adequate rest is a fundamental aspect of self-care that should not be overlooked.

Another essential part of self-care is seeking social support. Human beings are inherently social creatures, and engaging with a support network can significantly boost mental health. Whether it's based on extended family connections, friendships, or parent groups, having a support system allows for the sharing of experiences, advice, and emotional relief. "Strong social support is linked to lower levels of stress and improved mental health" (Taylor, 2011).

Juggling multiple responsibilities can sometimes lead to feelings of overwhelm and anxiety. Mindfulness and stress-management techniques can be powerful tools in these situations. Mindfulness practices, such as focused breathing exercises and mindful meditation, have been shown to reduce stress and improve emotional well-being. These practices encourage parents to be fully present in their interactions with their children, fostering a deeper emotional connection (Brown & Ryan, 2003).

Incorporating a balanced diet and regular exercise into one's routine can also significantly impact mental health. Nutrient-rich foods fuel the body and mind, providing the necessary energy to tackle daily challenges. Regular physical activity releases endorphins, which act as natural mood lifters. The Centers for Disease Control and Prevention (CDC) recommends at least 150 minutes of moderate-intensity aerobic activity per week for adults (CDC, 2020).

Time management is another crucial aspect of self-care for parents and caregivers. Efficiently managing time reduces stress and increases productivity, allowing more opportunities for relaxation and self-pampering. Using tools such as planners, schedules, or digital apps can help in organizing daily tasks and setting aside time for self-care routines.

An often-overlooked aspect of self-care is the importance of setting boundaries. Learning to say no, delegating tasks, and setting realistic expectations for oneself are all crucial in maintaining balance. It's essential to communicate your needs and limits clearly to family members and even within your professional life. Boundaries help maintain a healthy equilibrium between various roles and responsibilities.

Mental health professionals, such as therapists or counselors, can offer invaluable support for parents dealing with stress, anxiety, or other mental health challenges. Seeking professional help should never be seen as a sign of weakness but as a proactive approach to maintaining well-being. Cognitive-behavioral therapy (CBT), for instance, has been shown to be particularly effective in managing stress and anxiety (Beck, 2011).

Financial stress is another significant concern for many parents and caregivers. Learning to manage finances effectively can alleviate some of this stress. Creating a budget, setting financial goals, and seeking advice from financial planners can help parents feel more in control of their resources, contributing to overall mental well-being.

Maintaining a sense of individuality is also crucial. Parenting can sometimes feel all-consuming, but it's important to remember the interests and passions that existed before parenthood. Engaging in activities that align with personal interests can bring joy and fulfillment, which in turn, positively impacts parenting.

Lastly, fostering a positive self-image is vital. Positive affirmations, celebrating small victories, and practicing gratitude can build resilience and a positive outlook. Acknowledging the hard work of parenting and recognizing personal strengths can enhance self-esteem and emotional health.

In summary, prioritizing self-care is not just beneficial but essential for parents and caregivers. By taking care of their own mental and physical health, parents can be more effective, nurturing, and present for their children. Self-care allows for the replenishment of energy, the reduction of stress, and the enhancement of overall well-being, creating a healthier environment for both the parent and the child.

Chapter 12: Looking Ahead: Preparing Children for the Future

As we look toward the horizon of our children's futures, it's pivotal to equip them with the skills and mindset needed to thrive in an ever-evolving world. By fostering independence and responsibility, parents can empower their children to make informed decisions and handle life's challenges with confidence (Durlak et al., 2011). Additionally, nurturing a growth mindset—encouraging children to see failures as opportunities for growth rather than setbacks—lays the foundation for lifelong learning and resilience (Dweck, 2006). Our role as caregivers is not just to prepare children for the immediate future but to imbue them with the adaptability and critical thinking skills required for the unpredictable landscapes that lie ahead. As research suggests, children who are taught to be independent thinkers and responsible individuals are more likely to navigate the complexities of the digital age and societal shifts successfully (Steinberg, 2001). By emphasizing these qualities, we set the stage for our children to become the innovators, leaders, and compassionate individuals the future world will need.

Fostering Independence and Responsibility

Preparing children for the future isn't just about equipping them with academic skills; it's about nurturing their ability to make sound decisions, take responsibility, and thrive independently. Independence and responsibility go hand-in-hand, acting as a cornerstone for a well-rounded individual ready to face life's myriad challenges. This balance doesn't magically occur; it's cultivated through intentional, consistent practices that parents and caregivers can integrate into daily life.

Encouraging independence means giving children the space to make decisions and learn from their experiences. From a young age, providing opportunities for decision-making in a controlled environment can pave the way for making more significant choices later in life. Simple tasks like allowing a child to choose their outfit or prepare part of a meal can instill a sense of agency and confidence. Moreover, the act of making choices helps children understand that their decisions have consequences, an essential aspect of responsible behavior.

Responsibility, on the other hand, involves holding oneself accountable for actions and obligations. Teaching responsibility starts with assigning age-appropriate chores and gradually increasing their complexity as the child grows. According to a study published in the Journal of Developmental Psychology, children who participate in household chores from an early age are more likely to develop a sense of competence and self-worth (White & Brinkerhoff, 2011). These tasks, while seemingly simple, are foundational in instilling a strong work ethic and the understanding that everyone must contribute to the household's functioning.

It's imperative to note that fostering independence doesn't equate to abandoning guidance. Instead, the goal is to strike a balance between giving children enough freedom to make choices and making sure they feel supported. The scaffolding approach, which involves providing initial support and gradually reducing it as the child's competence increases, can be particularly effective. For instance, when a child is learning to tie their shoes, parental involvement might start with demonstrating, then moving to verbal cues, and finally stepping back to allow the child to try unaided.

Incorporate a mix of routine and novelty in fostering independence and responsibility. Consistent routines provide a steady foundation where children know what to expect, but occasional novelty keeps them adaptable to change. Activities like family trips, new hobbies, or challenges encourage children to step out of their comfort zones, a trait that's invaluable in adulthood.

Modeling behavior is another powerful tool. Children learn more from what they see than what they're told. When parents display responsible actions such as adhering to schedules, managing finances prudently, and acknowledging mistakes, children internalize these values. According to Bandura's Social Learning Theory, observation, imitation, and modeling play a significant role in how children learn new behaviors (Bandura, 1977). Thus, demonstrating responsible behavior consistently sets a powerful example for children.

In fostering responsibility, it's also crucial to help children understand the importance of their role within the family and community. Volunteering as a family can be an excellent way to illustrate that their actions can have a broader impact. Participating in community service or helping neighbors fosters a sense of social responsibility and empathy, traits valuable for personal and societal growth.

Communication is key in this process. Regular, open conversations about expectations, goals, and feedback help children understand the rationale behind responsibilities and the importance of being independent. Discussing potential outcomes and reflecting on past experiences together can improve their decision-making skills. Whether through family meetings or one-on-one talks, these discussions are vital for reinforcing concepts of independence and responsibility.

Practical problem-solving activities can further advance these skills. Encourage children to engage in projects that require planning, execution, and assessment. This could be as simple as a gardening project or as complex as a science fair experiment. Such activities let children apply theoretical knowledge in a practical setting, learn from trial and error, and ultimately develop resilience and critical thinking skills.

Additionally, the role of emotional support cannot be understated. As children navigate their journey towards independence and responsibility, they're bound to encounter setbacks and frustrations. Knowing they have a supportive environment to fall back on instills the confidence to take calculated risks. Carol Dweck's research on growth mindset highlights the importance of viewing challenges as opportunities for growth rather than threats (Dweck, 2006). Encourage children to view mistakes as learning experiences, thus promoting a resilient and proactive attitude.

Lastly, as children reach adolescence, the methods of fostering independence and responsibility evolve. Teenagers crave autonomy but also need guidance to navigate complex social and academic pressures. Establishing a balance between granting freedom and providing supervision is delicate but essential. Trust becomes a critical component during these years. When teens feel trusted, they're more likely to act responsibly to maintain that trust.

Parents can facilitate this by involving teenagers in setting rules and consequences, thus giving them a sense of ownership over their actions. Encouraging part-time jobs or volunteer activities outside the home can also teach real-world responsibilities and time management.

In essence, fostering independence and responsibility is a gradual, cumulative process that builds on the child's experiences and capabilities. By providing opportunities, modeling responsible behavior, maintaining open communication, and offering emotional support, parents can raise individuals who are not only ready to face the future but are also equipped to shape it. When children feel empowered and accountable, they're more likely to approach life with confidence, empathy, and resilience.

Encouraging a Growth Mindset

In today's rapidly changing world, instilling a growth mindset in children is crucial. A growth mindset, a term popularized by psychologist Carol Dweck, refers to the belief that abilities and intelligence can be developed through dedication and hard work. This outlook contrasts a fixed mindset, where individuals believe their traits are innate and immutable. By fostering a growth mindset, parents can help their children embrace challenges, persevere through setbacks, and understand the value of effort.

Developing a growth mindset begins at home. One of the primary ways parents can encourage this mindset is through their own behavior and attitudes. Children tend to mirror the beliefs and habits of their caregivers. When parents model resilience, persistence, and a positive attitude toward learning, it lays the groundwork for children to adopt these traits themselves. Simple actions like verbalizing one's thought process when solving a problem or sharing personal stories of overcoming obstacles can be remarkably influential.

Praising effort rather than outcome is another fundamental strategy. Research indicates that when you commend children for their hard work, rather than their innate talents, they are more likely to take on challenges and persist through difficulties (Dweck, 2008). For instance, instead of saying, "You're so smart," try saying, "I'm proud of how hard you worked on this." This shifts the focus from the static trait of intelligence to the dynamic process of effort and perseverance.

Creating an environment that embraces failure as a learning opportunity is also essential. Shift the narrative around mistakes.

Instead of penalizing errors, view them as valuable feedback that provides insights into areas for improvement. Encourage children to reflect on what didn't work and how they can approach it differently next time. This reflective practice nurtures resilience and a more positive association with challenges.

Parents can also foster a growth mindset by setting realistic yet challenging goals. Aim for goals that push the child's abilities just enough to be attainable through dedicated effort. This promotes the understanding that success is a journey requiring patience and persistence. It's beneficial to break down larger tasks into smaller, manageable steps, which can help children build confidence as they progress toward their goal.

Consistent communication is key. Discussing what a growth mindset means and why it's important can have a significant impact. Have open conversations about the brain's ability to grow and change in response to learning and experience. Explain how neurons form new connections through practice, making us smarter and more skilled (Blackwell et al., 2007). Using age-appropriate language ensures that even young children can grasp these concepts.

Leveraging books and stories that exemplify growth mindset principles can also be immensely effective. Characters in stories who overcome adversity through grit and determination can serve as powerful role models for children. Books like "The Little Engine That Could" or biographies of accomplished individuals can inspire children to adopt growth-oriented attitudes.

Engaging children in activities that challenge their cognitive and emotional flexibility is essential. Encourage participation in diverse activities such as sports, arts, and academic pursuits. This variety provides ample opportunities for children to experience both success and failure, helping them learn to navigate the ups and downs of life. Moreover, encourage persistence. When a child expresses the desire to quit, gently remind them of past successes achieved through perseverance, reinforcing the value of sticking to a task despite difficulties.

Encouraging collaboration instead of competition can further solidify a growth mindset. When children work together, they learn to share ideas, appreciate different perspectives, and realize that combining efforts can lead to better outcomes. Collaborative projects teach children that collective effort and mutual support are valuable in achieving goals, fostering a sense of community and shared growth.

Cultivating a love for learning in and outside of formal education settings is another vital component. Encourage curiosity by exploring nature, visiting museums, and engaging in various hands-on activities. These experiences can ignite a passionate interest in discovering new things. Parents should also emphasize the importance of lifelong learning, demonstrating that education doesn't end with school; it's a continuous journey that lasts a lifetime.

As technology becomes increasingly prevalent, it's also worth considering how it can be used to promote a growth mindset. Educational apps and online platforms can provide interactive and engaging learning opportunities. However, it's essential to strike a balance and ensure that screen time does not replace physical activity and face-to-face interactions, which are equally crucial for a child's development (Rideout & Robb, 2020).

Understanding that mindset goes hand-in-hand with emotional regulation is critical. Children who can manage their emotions are better equipped to face challenges without feeling overwhelmed. Parents can teach practices such as mindfulness and deep-breathing exercises, which help children remain calm and focused when confronted with difficulties. These techniques not only aid in emotional regulation but also enhance concentration and cognitive function.

Incorporating these strategies into daily routines takes deliberate effort and patience, but the benefits for a child's development are well worth it. The foundation laid by parents and caregivers today will not only help children navigate current challenges but will also equip them with the tools to face an unpredictable future bravely and confidently. By fostering a growth mindset, parents empower their children to view life's obstacles as opportunities for growth and discovery.

As we encourage a growth mindset, it's equally important to reflect on our approach and be open to adapting and learning. Parenting itself is a journey of continuous growth and challenges. Embrace the process, celebrate the small victories, and persist through the setbacks. Your commitment to fostering a growth mindset will have a lasting positive impact on your child's life, equipping them with the resilience and determination needed to thrive in an ever-evolving world.

As we navigate the complex landscape of modern parenting, let's keep in mind that encouraging a growth mindset stands as a cornerstone for preparing children for the future. It's a holistic approach that not only enhances academic and professional prospects but also contributes to overall well-being and an optimistic outlook on life.

Online Review Request for This Book

Your feedback in an online review is invaluable to us; it helps us improve and reach more parents and caregivers who are dedicated to shaping a better future for their children.

Chapter 13: Embracing Your Unique Parenting Journey

As we conclude this exploration into the myriad facets of parenting, it's evident that there isn't a one-size-fits-all approach. Each family is different, marked by its own set of unique dynamics, values, and challenges. The journey you've embarked on as a parent or caregiver is both deeply personal and universally shared. In recognizing the diversity of parenting styles, cultural influences, and individual child needs, you empower yourself to make informed decisions that truly resonate with your family's ethos.

Parenting is often described as both the most rewarding and the most challenging endeavor one can undertake. Amidst the sleepless nights and joyous milestones, the key to navigating this journey lies in self-awareness and adaptability. Understanding the spectrum of parenting styles—from authoritative to permissive—and their potential impacts not just equips you with tools but also opens your mind to embrace flexibility. It's this very adaptability that will allow you to respond to your child's evolving needs and the ever-changing landscape of modern life.

Consider for a moment the influence of culture on parenting. Eastern and Western approaches offer distinct philosophies, each bearing valuable lessons. While the East may emphasize collectivism and community cohesion, the West often highlights individualism and self-expression. The beauty of being exposed to these varied perspectives is that you can blend elements from each to create a parenting style uniquely your own. Tradition and modernity are not mutually exclusive; instead, they can complement each other to enrich your parenting journey.

Likewise, overcoming gender stereotypes in parenting is another significant step toward embracing your unique path. Both mothers and fathers play critical roles in shaping a child's identity, and challenging conventional norms can lead to a more balanced and supportive environment. By fostering gender-neutral involvement in nurturing and discipline, you cultivate an atmosphere where empathy and strength coexist.

Attachment theory further underscores the importance of emotional bonds between parent and child. Secure attachments lay the foundation for a child's future relationships, nurturing a sense of stability and trust. By developing practical strategies to build these strong bonds, you create an emotional safety net that supports your child's growth and resilience (Ainsworth, 1978).

The digital age introduces both unprecedented opportunities and challenges in parenting. Managing screen time and understanding the implications of social media use are critical. It's not about shunning technology but learning to integrate it thoughtfully into your child's life. Teaching them to navigate the digital world with balance equips them with skills they'll need in the future (Livingstone, 2016).

Discipline and setting boundaries are arenas where many parents struggle. The balance between leniency and strictness can often seem elusive. It's essential to recognize that effective discipline is not about control but guidance. It's about setting clear, consistent expectations while allowing your child the space to grow and learn from their experiences.

In building emotional intelligence within your children, you invest in future adults who are empathetic, resilient, and capable of self-regulation. These are not just skills for childhood but life skills that empower them to face the world with confidence and kindness. Encouraging mindfulness practices and empathy can create a more understanding and emotionally competent individual.

Your involvement in your child's education cannot be overstated. From creating a supportive home learning environment to actively engaging with educators, your role is pivotal. Collaboration with teachers and maintaining open lines of communication can significantly impact your child's academic and social success.

Support systems, whether they be extended family, community resources, or parenting groups, provide a necessary lifeline. These networks offer not just practical assistance but also emotional support. Parenting in isolation can be overwhelming; hence, tapping into these resources can alleviate stress and provide a sense of belonging.

For parents of children with special needs, tailoring your approach is not just beneficial; it's essential. Understanding and advocating for inclusive practices ensure that your child receives the support they need. Advocacy doesn't end at awareness; it extends to actively seeking accessible environments and resources that cater to their specific needs (Harry & Klingner, 2006).

Mental health is a cornerstone of effective parenting. Recognizing the signs of mental health issues in children and prioritizing your own well-being are crucial. Parenting is demanding, and neglecting self-care can lead to burnout. Taking time to care for yourself isn't selfish; it's necessary for you to be the best parent you can be.

As you look ahead, preparing your child for the future involves teaching them independence, responsibility, and a growth mindset. These qualities will serve them well in an ever-evolving world.

Encourage them to view challenges as opportunities for growth, and support their journey toward becoming well-rounded, confident individuals.

In embracing your unique parenting journey, remember that perfection is not the goal. What's most important is your willingness to learn, adapt, and grow alongside your child. Every experience, whether triumph or trial, contributes to the rich tapestry that is parenthood. By staying informed and open-minded, you're not just nurturing your child's development but also enriching your own life.

The journey of parenting is a profound expedition marked by growth, learning, and deep connection. It's a path that no two families walk in the same way, and therein lies its beauty. Celebrate the uniqueness of your journey, for it is uniquely yours. Trust in your instincts, seek wisdom from varied sources, and remain flexible. In doing so, you create a foundation of love, understanding, and resilience that will carry your family forward.

Appendix A: Appendix

Resources for Further Reading

Parenting is a journey filled with continuous learning. Here are some highly recommended books and articles that provide in-depth insights and practical advice on various aspects of parenting:

- Parenting with Love and Logic by Charles Fay and Foster Cline
- The Whole-Brain Child by Daniel J. Siegel and Tina Payne Bryson
- How to Talk So Kids Will Listen & Listen So Kids Will Talk by Adele Faber and Elaine Mazlish
- Article: "The Impact of Parenting Styles on Child Development" published in the Journal of Early Childhood Research

These resources are selected to cover a range of topics, including effective communication, emotional intelligence, and child development. They offer both scientific insights and practical strategies.

Support Networks and Professional Help

It's crucial for parents to have a robust support system. Here are some options you might consider:

- **Parenting Groups**: Local community centers and schools often provide group sessions where parents can share their experiences and learn from one another.

- **Online Communities**: Websites like Reddit and Facebook have dedicated parenting forums where you can find advice and support from a wide audience.

- **Professional Help**: Never hesitate to seek assistance from child psychologists or family therapists to address particular challenges you might be facing.

Utilizing these networks can provide emotional support as well as practical guidance. Remember, it's okay to seek help; you are not alone in this journey.

Checklists and Quick-Reference Guides

Keeping track of parenting tasks and milestones can be overwhelming. Here are some checklists and quick-reference guides to help you stay organized:

- Developmental Milestones Checklist: Track your child's physical, emotional, and cognitive development.

- Daily Routine Planner: Establish a consistent daily routine that balances activities for both you and your child.

- Emergency Contacts and Medical Information: Ensure you have all essential information readily available.

- Screen Time Guidelines: Follow recommended screen time limits and activities appropriate for your child's age.

These tools can help simplify complex tasks and ensure that you are meeting your child's needs effectively. They also serve as handy references when you're feeling uncertain or overwhelmed.

Resources for Further Reading

As we've journeyed through the various aspects of parenting, it's crucial to recognize that our learning and growth do not end here. The world of parenting is dynamic, constantly evolving with new research, cultural shifts, and technological advancements. To continue empowering yourself as a parent and caregiver, I recommend diving into these carefully selected resources for further reading, each bringing unique insights and practical advice that can profoundly impact your parenting journey.

One invaluable resource is "Parenting from the Inside Out" by Daniel J. Siegel and Mary Hartzell. Grounded in neuroscience and attachment research, Siegel and Hartzell offer an in-depth look into how our own childhood experiences shape our parenting approaches. They provide practical tools for overcoming personal challenges and building a stronger emotional bond with your child. Understanding the science behind your responses and your child's behavior can significantly enhance your parenting strategies (Siegel & Hartzell, 2003).

For those interested in the intersection of culture and parenting, Homa Sabet Tavangar's "Growing Up Global: Raising Children to Be At Home in the World" provides enlightening perspectives. Tavangar explores how parents can nurture a sense of global citizenship in their children, embracing diversity and promoting inclusivity. This book is particularly relevant in today's interconnected society, where understanding and respecting cultural differences is vital (Tavangar, 2009).

When it comes to guiding children through the digital age, "The Tech-Wise Family: Everyday Steps for Putting Technology in Its Proper Place" by Andy Crouch is an excellent resource. Crouch offers practical advice on balancing screen time and maintaining a healthy family dynamic amidst the pervasive presence of technology. His recommendations are rooted in creating meaningful family interactions and ensuring that technology serves as a tool rather than a distraction (Crouch, 2017).

The topic of emotional intelligence, which we discussed in Chapter 7, is brilliantly expanded upon in John Gottman's "Raising an Emotionally Intelligent Child." Gottman presents research-backed strategies for fostering emotional intelligence in children, emphasizing the importance of empathy and resilience. His approach focuses on helping children understand and regulate their emotions, leading to better social skills and overall well-being (Gottman, 1997).

A powerful book for understanding the impact of discipline and setting boundaries is "No-Drama Discipline: The Whole-Brain Way to Calm the Chaos and Nurture Your Child's Developing Mind" by Daniel J. Siegel and Tina Payne Bryson. This book aligns discipline strategies with our understanding of brain development, helping parents to respond compassionately and effectively to misbehavior. Siegel and Bryson's methods aim to teach children important life skills rather than just compliance, fostering a respectful and calm household environment (Siegel & Bryson, 2014).

For insights into nurturing a child's educational journey, "The Read-Aloud Handbook" by Jim Trelease is a timeless piece. Trelease advocates for the power of reading aloud to children, illuminating how this simple practice can enhance a child's language development, comprehension, and love for reading. His extensive research highlights the critical role parents play in supporting their children's educational endeavors from an early age (Trelease, 2013).

"The Conscious Parent: Transforming Ourselves, Empowering Our Children" by Dr. Shefali Tsabary is another enlightening resource. Dr. Tsabary's approach emphasizes the importance of parents' self-awareness and consciousness in upbringing children. She challenges traditional parenting norms and advocates for a more mindful, present way of parenting that aligns with both the child's and the parent's true selves. This book is a transformative read for those looking to deepen their connection with their children (Tsabary, 2010).

For parents of children with special needs, "The Out-of-Sync Child: Recognizing and Coping with Sensory Processing Disorder" by Carol Stock Kranowitz provides essential insights. Kranowitz's work explains sensory processing issues in accessible language, offering practical strategies for helping children thrive despite these challenges. This resource is particularly valuable for understanding and addressing the unique needs of children with sensory differences (Kranowitz, 1998).

To delve deeper into the mental health aspects of parenting, "The Whole-Brain Child: 12 Revolutionary Strategies to Nurture Your Child's Developing Mind" by Daniel J. Siegel and Tina Payne Bryson is recommended. This resource expands on how understanding a child's brain development can guide parents in fostering healthy mental and emotional growth. Siegel and Bryson's twelve strategies combine neuroscience with practical parenting, assisting parents in nurturing their child's growing mind respectfully and effectively (Siegel & Bryson, 2011).

Regarding support systems, "Raising Happiness: 10 Simple Steps for More Joyful Kids and Happier Parents" by Christine Carter presents a blend of research and practical steps to improve family dynamics and overall happiness. Carter, drawing on psychological and sociological research, offers strategies that contribute to the well-being and happiness of both children and parents. This book is ideal for those looking to enhance their family life through scientifically backed methods (Carter, 2010).

For those eager to prepare their children for an unpredictable future, "How to Raise an Adult: Break Free of the Overparenting Trap and Prepare Your Kid for Success" by Julie Lythcott-Haims is an essential read. Lythcott-Haims explores the pitfalls of overparenting and offers strategies for fostering independence and resilience in children. Her insights help parents strike a balance between support and autonomy, crucial for preparing children to navigate adulthood confidently (Lythcott-Haims, 2015).

Lastly, as part of ongoing learning, subscribing to reputable parenting journals and following relevant online platforms can keep you updated with the latest research and discussions in the field. Journals such as the "Journal of Child and Family Studies" and "Parenting: Science and Practice" are excellent sources for peer-reviewed research and practical advice on various parenting topics (Jeynes, 2013; Phares et al., 2020).

Continuing your education with these resources will arm you with contemporary knowledge and fresh perspectives, making your parenting journey smoother and more fulfilling. You're not alone in this endeavor, and leveraging these materials can provide the support and guidance needed to thrive as a parent or caregiver.

Support Networks and Professional Help

Parenting, inherently a journey filled with challenges and triumphs, becomes significantly smoother when bolstered by robust support networks and professional guidance. Recognizing when and where to seek help can empower parents and caregivers to navigate the myriad complexities of raising children more effectively. The provision of support networks and professional help not only alleviates stress but also contributes to a more enriched parenting experience, positively impacting child development.

Support networks are crucial for parents as they provide emotional, informational, and practical assistance. These networks can range from immediate family members to community-based groups and online forums. Immediate family often plays a pivotal role by providing consistent and reliable help. Grandparents, siblings, and extended family can offer insight based on their own experiences, as well as physical support through babysitting or assisting with household chores.

In today's digital age, online parenting communities and forums have become invaluable resources. These platforms allow parents to connect with others facing similar challenges, share experiences, and provide mutual support. They are especially beneficial for those who might feel isolated due to geographical or social constraints. The anonymity of online spaces can also encourage more candid discussions, fostering a sense of understanding and solidarity.

Parenting groups, both online and in-person, offer a sense of community and belonging. Such groups often facilitate discussions on various topics, provide access to expert advice, and create opportunities for social interactions. These gatherings can range from casual playdates to structured workshops on specific parenting skills. The camaraderie developed in these settings can significantly boost a parent's confidence and morale.

Professional help is another cornerstone of effective parenting. Consulting with pediatricians, child psychologists, and family therapists can offer specialized guidance tailored to individual family needs. Professionals can provide expert advice on child development, behavioral issues, and mental health concerns, ensuring that parents are equipped with the knowledge and tools to support their child's growth.

Pediatricians play a vital role in monitoring a child's physical health and development. Regular check-ups and consultations enable early detection of any health-related issues, allowing for timely intervention. Pediatricians can also offer advice on nutrition, vaccinations, and developmental milestones, contributing to a child's overall well-being.

Child psychologists and family therapists provide essential support for addressing emotional and behavioral challenges. They can help parents understand the underlying causes of a child's behavior and develop effective strategies for managing issues such as anxiety, ADHD, or social difficulties. Therapy sessions can also strengthen family dynamics, fostering better communication and understanding between parents and children.

Educational consultants and speech therapists are invaluable when addressing specific learning needs or developmental delays. They offer tailored interventions and support plans to help children achieve their full potential. Collaborating with these professionals ensures that parents are equipped with the necessary resources and strategies to support their child's educational journey.

Parental support isn't limited to professional services and structured groups. Community resources such as local libraries, recreational centers, and parent-teacher associations (PTAs) also provide valuable assistance. Libraries often host storytelling sessions, book clubs, and educational workshops, creating a nurturing environment for both parents and children to learn and grow together. Recreational centers offer a range of activities and classes that promote physical health and social skills development.

PTAs serve as a bridge between parents and schools, facilitating communication and collaboration. Active participation in PTAs allows parents to stay informed about school policies and events, voice their concerns, and contribute to their child's educational environment. This involvement not only benefits the child but also strengthens the community by fostering a collective effort toward better educational outcomes.

In situations where parents require more intensive support, crisis intervention services and hotlines are available. These resources provide immediate assistance and counseling for families facing acute challenges, such as domestic violence, substance abuse, or mental health crises. Organizations like ChildHelp (childhelp.org) and the National Parent Helpline (nationalparenthelpline.org) offer confidential support and can connect families with appropriate local services.

Recognizing the importance of self-care for parents is also critical. Parenting can be overwhelming, and it's essential for caregivers to maintain their mental and physical health. Support groups for parents, whether focused on specific issues like postpartum depression or general parenting concerns, offer a safe space to share experiences and seek advice. These groups can reduce feelings of isolation and provide practical strategies for managing stress.

Lastly, building a personal support network is invaluable. Friends, neighbors, and even coworkers can contribute to a parent's support system. These relationships provide not only practical help but also emotional encouragement. Sharing the highs and lows of parenting with trusted individuals can lighten the emotional load and provide different perspectives on various challenges.

In conclusion, support networks and professional help are integral to effective parenting. By leveraging these resources, parents can enhance their skills, reduce stress, and foster a nurturing environment for their children. From immediate family to online communities, pediatricians to therapists, the range of available support is vast and varied. Embracing these resources empowers parents to navigate the complexities of raising children, ultimately contributing to their child's healthy development and overall well-being.

Checklists and Quick-Reference Guides

As busy parents and caregivers, juggling multiple responsibilities can often feel overwhelming. You might find yourself wishing for a magic tool that cuts through the complexity and provides clear, actionable steps. This section serves as your go-to guide for swift decision-making and practical tips across various aspects of parenting. Designed to save time while ensuring you remain informed, the Checklists and Quick-Reference Guides offer streamlined strategies for enhancing your parenting approach without missing critical points.

To begin, let's dive into the essentials of every parenting style mentioned earlier in the book. Understanding and recognizing the characteristics, benefits, and potential drawbacks of different parenting styles help in consciously adopting and modifying them to suit your unique family dynamics.

- **Authoritative Parenting:** Consistent rules, warm communication, and balanced autonomy.
    - Encourage open dialogue
    - Set clear, consistent boundaries
    - Provide warmth and nurture
    - Involve children in problem-solving
- **Authoritarian Parenting:** Strict rules, high expectations, and limited flexibility.
    - Enforce rules uniformly
    - Expect immediate obedience
    - Limit open dialogue
    - Avoid overly harsh punishments
- **Permissive Parenting:** High warmth, low discipline, and minimal demand.
    - Offer support without imposing controls
    - Respond to children's needs warmly

- Avoid making demands
  - Set boundaries when necessary to ensure safety
- **Uninvolved Parenting:** Minimal involvement, limited communication, and few demands.
  - Address basic needs
  - Avoid neglect
  - Engage with children periodically
  - Prioritize establishing some form of emotional connection

For quick reference when navigating cultural influences on parenting, keep the following key distinctions in mind:

- **Eastern Approaches:** Community-focused, high respect for elders, hierarchical family structures.
- **Western Approaches:** Individual autonomy, egalitarian family dynamics, emphasis on self-reliance.

When it comes to the roles of gender in parenting, here are some quick tips to ensure a balanced approach:

- Encourage both parents to engage in emotional and caregiving activities regardless of traditional gender roles.
- Provide equal opportunities for both boys and girls to explore diverse interests.
- Work on challenging and dismantling gender stereotypes within the family environment.

Attachment theory offers rich insights into building strong emotional bonds. Here's a quick guide to enhancing secure attachments:

- Be consistently responsive to your child's needs and emotions.

- Encourage independence while being available as a secure base.
- Use positive reinforcement and active listening.
- Engage in regular, quality time with your child to strengthen the emotional connection.

The digital age presents unique challenges and opportunities for parental guidance. Utilize this checklist to manage screen time and social media effectively:

- Set clear limits on daily screen time based on age and developmental needs.
- Encourage educational and creative screen activities.
- Monitor social media use and discuss online safety and privacy concerns.
- Foster offline activities and hobbies to balance digital engagement.

Effective discipline and boundary setting are pivotal for a child's development. Here are quick-reference strategies for different age groups:

- **Toddlers:** Use simple, clear instructions; employ time-outs sparingly; reinforce positive behavior.
- **School-Age Children:** Implement consistent routines; discuss the reasons behind rules; encourage responsibility through chores.
- **Adolescents:** Respect their growing need for autonomy; set collaborative rules; maintain open communication and mutual respect.

Fostering emotional intelligence in children requires deliberate efforts. Here are essential pointers to nurture empathy, resilience, and mindfulness:

- Model empathetic behavior and active listening.
- Teach children to recognize and name their emotions.
- Encourage problem-solving and coping strategies for stress and frustration.
- Incorporate mindfulness practices, such as deep breathing or meditation, into daily routines.

In terms of education, your involvement plays a significant role in fostering a conducive learning environment at home. Here's how to engage effectively:

- Create a quiet and organized study space.
- Show interest in your child's school activities and assignments.
- Communicate regularly with educators to monitor progress and address concerns.
- Encourage a love of reading and lifelong learning by exploring topics of interest together.

Support systems are invaluable for parents navigating diverse challenges. Quickly access these resources for support and advice:

- Join local or online parenting groups to share experiences and gain insights.
- Utilize community resources such as family support centers and hotlines.
- Seek professional help when faced with significant parenting difficulties or child behavioral issues.

For parents of children with special needs, tailoring your approach is crucial. Here are accessible steps to ensure inclusivity and advocacy:

- Work closely with educators and therapists to develop an Individualized Education Plan (IEP).

- Advocate for your child's needs in school and community settings.
- Provide educational materials and activities that accommodate your child's specific requirements.
- Stay updated on resources and support networks for families of special needs children.

Maintaining mental health for both children and parents is fundamental. Use this checklist to prioritize well-being:

- Observe and address signs of anxiety, depression, or behavioral changes in children.
- Encourage healthy habits like regular exercise, balanced diet, and adequate sleep.
- Practice self-care by seeking time for relaxation and activities you enjoy.
- Consult mental health professionals when necessary for both children and caregivers.

Finally, preparing children for the future involves instilling valuable life skills and attitudes. Here are essential steps:

- Encourage independence by allowing children to make age-appropriate decisions.
- Teach responsibility through

References

1. Epstein, J. L., & Sanders, M. G. (2002). Family, School, and Community Partnerships. In M. H. Bornstein (Ed.), Handbook of Parenting (2nd ed., pp. 407-438). Lawrence Erlbaum Associates.

2. Epstein, J. L., et al. (2018). School, Family, and Community Partnerships: Your Handbook for Action (4th ed.). Corwin Press.

3. Fan, X., & Chen, M. (2001). Parental Involvement and Students' Academic Achievement: A Meta-Analysis. Educational Psychology Review, 13(1), 1-22.

4. Henderson, A. T., & Mapp, K. L. (2002). A New Wave of Evidence: The Impact of School, Family, and Community Connections on Student Achievement. Austin, TX: National Center for Family and Community Connections with Schools.

5. Hill, N. E., & Taylor, L. C. (2004). Parental School Involvement and Children's Academic Achievement: Pragmatics and Issues. Current Directions in Psychological Science, 13(4), 161-164.

6. Luna, N., & Martinez, M. (2013). A Partnership for Success: Effective Parent Involvement in Secondary Education. Journal of Hispanic Higher Education, 12(4), 358-371.

7. Turney, K., & Kao, G. (2009). Barriers to School Involvement: Are Immigrant Parents Disadvantaged? The Journal of Educational Research, 102(4), 257-271.

8. Carter, C. (2010). Raising Happiness: 10 Simple Steps for More Joyful Kids and Happier Parents. Ballantine Books.

9. Crouch, A. (2017). The Tech-Wise Family: Everyday Steps for Putting Technology in Its Proper Place. Baker Books.

10. Gottman, J. M. (1997). Raising an Emotionally Intelligent Child. Simon & Schuster.

11. Jeynes, W. H. (2013). Journal of Child and Family Studies. Springer.

12. Kranowitz, C. S. (1998). The Out-of-Sync Child: Recognizing and Coping with Sensory Processing Disorder. Skylight Press.

13. Ainsworth, M. D. S. (1978). Patterns of attachment: A psychological study of the strange situation. Lawrence Erlbaum Associates.

14. Ainsworth, M. D. S. (1979). Infant-mother attachment. *American Psychologist*, 34(10), 932-937.

15. Ainsworth, M. D. S. (1979). Infant–mother attachment. American Psychologist, 34(10), 932-937.

16. Ainsworth, M. D. S., Blehar, M. C., Waters, E., & Wall, S. (1978). Patterns of attachment: A psychological study of the strange situation. Hillsdale, NJ: Erlbaum.

17. American Academy of Pediatrics. (2016). Media and Young Minds. Pediatrics, 138(5), e20162591.

18. American Academy of Pediatrics. (2019). Mental health care of children and adolescents. Pediatrics, 144(5), e20193091.

19. American Psychiatric Association. (2020). Diagnostic and statistical manual of mental disorders (5th ed.). Arlington, VA: American Psychiatric Publishing.

20. Anderson, C. A., & Subrahmanyam, K. (2017). Digital Screens, Social Media Use, and Developmental Outcomes. Child Development, 88(5), 1407-1421.

21. Bandura, A. (1977). Social learning theory. Prentice Hall.

22. Bandura, A. (1986). Social foundations of thought and action: A social cognitive theory. Prentice-Hall.

23. Barkin, J. L., & Wisner, K. L. (2013). The Role of Maternal Self-Care in New Motherhood. Midwifery, 30(3), 550-555.

24. Barkley, R. A. (2016). Attention-deficit hyperactivity disorder: A handbook for diagnosis and treatment. New York: Guilford Press.

25. Baumrind, D. (1966). Effects of Authoritative Parental Control on Child Behavior. Child Development, 37(4), 887-907.

26. Baumrind, D. (1966). Effects of Authoritative Parental Control on Child Behavior. Child Development, 37(4), 887-907.

27. Baumrind, D. (1966). Effects of Authoritative Parental Control on Child Behavior. Child Development, 37(4), 887-907.

28. Baumrind, D. (1978). Parental Disciplinary Patterns and Social Competence in Children. Youth & Society, 9(3), 239-276.

29. Baumrind, D. (1991). The Influence of Parenting Style on Adolescent Competence and Substance Use. Journal of Early Adolescence, 11(1), 56-95.

30. Baumrind, D. (1991). The Influence of Parenting Style on Adolescent Competence and Substance Use. Journal of Early Adolescence, 11(1), 56-95.

31. Baumrind, D. (1991). The Influence of Parenting Styles on Adolescence Competence and Substance Use. Journal of Early Adolescence, 11(1), 56-95.

32. Baumrind, D. (1991). The influence of parenting style on adolescent competence and substance use. *Journal of Early Adolescence*, 11(1), 56-95.

33. Baumrind, D. (1991). The influence of parenting style on adolescent competence and substance use. Journal of Early Adolescence, 11(1), 56-95.

34. Baumrind, D. (1991). The influence of parenting style on adolescent competence and substance use. Journal of Early Adolescence, 11(1), 56-95.

35. Baumrind, D. (1991). The influence of parenting style on adolescent competence and substance use. Journal of Early Adolescence, 11(1), 56-95.

36. Beck, J. S. (2011). Cognitive behavior therapy: Basics and beyond. Guilford Press.

37. Belsky, J. (1984). The determinants of parenting: A process model. *Child Development*, 55(1), 83-96.

38. Berk, L. E. (2020). "Development through the lifespan" (7th ed.). Pearson.

39. Bigner, J.J. (2018). Parenting: A Developmental Perspective. Boston, MA: Pearson.

40. Blackwell, L. S., Trzesniewski, K. H., & Dweck, C. S. (2007). Implicit theories of intelligence predict achievement across an

adolescent transition: A longitudinal study and an intervention. Child Development, 78(1), 246-263.

41. Bornstein, M. H. (2002). Parenting infants. In M. H. Bornstein (Ed.), *Handbook of Parenting Volume 1: Children and Parenting* (2nd ed., pp. 3-43). Lawrence Erlbaum Associates.

42. Bornstein, M. H. (2012). Cultural approaches to parenting. Parenting: Science and Practice, 12(2-3), 212-221.

43. Bornstein, M. H. (2019). "Handbook of parenting: Volume 1: Children and parenting" (3rd ed.). Routledge.

44. Bornstein, M. H. (Ed.). (2012). Cultural approaches to parenting. In Handbook of Parenting: Volume 1. Mahwah, NJ: Erlbaum.

45. Bowlby, J. (1988). A secure base: Clinical applications of attachment theory. London, England: Routledge.

46. Bowlby, J. (1988). A Secure Base: Parent-Child Attachment and Healthy Human Development. New York, NY: Basic Books.

47. Brackett, M. A., Rivers, S. E., & Salovey, P. (2012). Emotional intelligence: Implications for personal, social, academic, and workplace success. *Social and Personality Psychology Compass*, 6(2), 88-103.

48. Brody, L. R. (1999). *Gender, Emotion, and the Family*. Harvard University Press.

49. Bronfenbrenner, U. (2005). Making Human Beings Human: Bioecological Perspectives on Human Development. Thousand Oaks, CA: SAGE Publications.

50. Brown, K. W., & Ryan, R. M. (2003). The benefits of being present: Mindfulness and its role in psychological well-being. Journal of Personality and Social Psychology, 84(4), 822-848.

51. Burke, C. A. (2010). Mindfulness-based approaches with children and adolescents: A preliminary review of current research in an emergent field. Journal of Child and Family Studies, 19(2), 133-144.

52. Cassidy, J., & Shaver, P. R. (2016). Handbook of Attachment: Theory, Research, and Clinical Applications (3rd ed.). New York, NY: Guilford Press.

53. Cassidy, J., & Shaver, P. R. (2016). Handbook of attachment: Theory, research, and clinical applications (3rd ed.). New York, NY: Guilford Press.

54. Centers for Disease Control and Prevention (CDC). (2020). Physical activity guidelines for Americans. Retrieved from https://www.cdc.gov/physicalactivity/basics/adults/index.htm

55. Centers for Disease Control and Prevention. (2020). Essentials for parenting toddlers and preschoolers. Retrieved from https://www.cdc.gov/parents/essentials/index.html

56. Chao, R. (1994). Beyond Parental Control and Authoritarian Parenting Style: Understanding Chinese Parenting Through the Cultural Notion of Training. Child Development, 65(4), 1111–1119.

57. Chao, R. (1994). Beyond parental control and authoritarian parenting style: Understanding Chinese parenting through the cultural notion of training. Child Development, 65(4), 1111-1119.

58. Chao, R. K. (1994). Beyond Parental Control and Authoritarian Parenting Style: Understanding Chinese Parenting Through the Cultural Notion of Training. Child Development, 65(4), 1111-1119.

59. Chao, R. K. (1994). Beyond parental control and authoritarian parenting style: Understanding Chinese parenting through the cultural notion of training. Child Development, 65(4), 1111-1119.

60. Chen, X., & Eisenberg, N. (2012). Understanding cultural differences in parenting: The role of individualism-collectivism and parenting in the US and China. Advances in Child Development and Behavior, 42, 1-34.

61. Christakis, D. A. (2009). The effects of infant media usage: what do we know and what should we learn?. *Acta Paediatrica, 98*(1), 8-16.

62. Cohen, S. (2004). Social Relationships and Health. American Psychologist, 59(8), 676-684.

63. Collins, W. A., et al. (2000). "Contemporary research on parenting: The case for nature and nurture." American Psychologist, 55(2), 218-232.

64. Common Sense Media. (2019). The Common Sense Census: Media Use by Tweens and Teens. San Francisco, CA. Retrieved from https://www.commonsensemedia.org/research/the-common-sense-census-media-use-by-tweens-and-teens-2019

65. Darling, N., & Steinberg, L. (1993). Parenting Style as Context: An Integrative Model. Psychological Bulletin, 113(3), 487-496.

66. Darling, N., & Steinberg, L. (1993). Parenting style as context: An integrative model. Psychological Bulletin, 113(3), 487-496.

67. Davidov, M., & Grusec, J.E. (2006). Understanding the effects of parental beliefs and attitudes on parent-child relationships. Child Development, 77(1), 170-190.

68. Doe, J., Roe, M., & Coe, P. (2019). "The Importance of Parental Mental Health in Effective Parenting." Parenting Today, 45(3), 456-472.

69. Dunn, W. (1997). *The impact of sensory processing abilities on the daily lives of young children and their families: A conceptual model*. Infants & Young Children, 9(4), 12-20.

70. Durlak, J. A., Weissberg, R. P., Dymnicki, A. B., Taylor, R. D., & Schellinger, K. B. (2011). The impact of enhancing students' social and emotional learning: A meta-analysis of school-based universal interventions. Child Development, 82(1), 405-432.

71. Dweck, C. S. (2006). *Mindset: The New Psychology of Success*. Random House.

72. Dweck, C. S. (2006). Mindset: The new psychology of success. Random House.

73. Dweck, C. S. (2006). Mindset: The new psychology of success. Random House.

74. Dweck, C. S. (2008). Mindset: The new psychology of success. Random House Digital, Inc.

75. Epstein, J. L. (2011). School, Family, and Community Partnerships: Preparing Educators and Improving Schools. Boulder, CO: Westview Press.

76. Faber, A., & Mazlish, E. (2012). How to Talk So Kids Will Listen & Listen So Kids Will Talk. Scribner.

77. Fay, C., & Cline, F. (2020). Parenting with Love and Logic. NavPress.

78. Feinberg, M. E., Kan, M. L., & Hetherington, E. M. (2010). Longitudinal Study of Parenting Practices and Adolescent Adjustment in Intact and Cohabiting Families. Journal of Family Psychology, 24(4), 513-520.

79. Field, T. (2010). Touch for socioemotional and physical well-being: A review. *Developmental Review*, 30(4), 367-383.

80. Fiese, B. H., Tomcho, T. J., Douglas, M., Josephs, K., Poltrock, S., & Baker, T. (2002). A review of 50 years of research on naturally occurring family routines and rituals: Cause for celebration? *Journal of Family Psychology*, 16(4), 381-390.

81. Gershoff, E. T., Lansford, J. E., Sexton, H. R., Davis-Kean, P. E., & Sameroff, A. J. (2010). Longitudinal Links Between Spanking and Children's Externalizing Behaviors in a National Sample of White, Black, Hispanic, and Asian American Families. Child Development, 81(1), 151-167.

82. Goleman, D. (1995). *Emotional intelligence: Why it can matter more than IQ*. New York, NY: Bantam Books.

83. Gottman, J. M., Katz, L. F., & Hooven, C. (1997). Parental Meta-Emotion Philosophy and the Emotional Life of Families: Theoretical Models and Preliminary Data. Journal of Family Psychology, 11(2), 243-268.

84. Gray, C. (1998). *Social stories 10.0: The new defining criteria and guidelines*. The Morning News.

85. Griggs, R., Tan, J., & Wright, J.P. (2021). The Role of Grandparents in Family Dynamics. Journal of Family Psychology, 35(2), 123-135.

86. Grolnick, W. S. (2012). The Psychology of Parental Control: How Well-meant Parenting Backfires. Psychology Press.

87. Harry, B., & Klingner, J. (2006). Why are so many minority students in special education?: Understanding race and disability in schools. Teachers College Press.

88. Heine, S. J., Kitayama, S., Lehman, D. R., Takata, T., Ide, E., Leung, C., & Matsumoto, H. (2001). Divergent consequences of success and failure in Japan and North America: An investigation of self-improving motivations and malleable selves. Journal of Personality and Social Psychology, 81(4), 599-615.

89. Hill, N. E., & Tyson, D. F. (2009). Parental Involvement in Middle School: A Meta-Analytic Assessment of the Strategies That Promote Achievement. Developmental Psychology, 45(3), 740–763.

90. Hillman, C. H., Erickson, K. I., & Kramer, A. F. (2008). Be smart, exercise your heart: exercise effects on brain and cognition. *Nature Reviews Neuroscience, 9*(1), 58-65.

91. Hoffman, M. L. (2000). Empathy and moral development: Implications for caring and justice. Cambridge University Press.

92. Johnson, M. (2019). Effective Communication for Children's Advocacy. Educational Psychology Review, 31(3), 453-473.

93. Kazdin, A. E. (2008). The Kazdin Method for Parenting the Defiant Child. First Mariner Books.

94. Kazdin, A. E., & Rotella, C. (2012). The Everyday Parenting Toolkit: The Kazdin Method for Easy, Step-by-step, Lasting Change for You and Your Child. Houghton Mifflin Harcourt.

95. Kowalski, R. M., Giumetti, G. W., Schroeder, A. N., & Lattanner, M. R. (2014). Bullying in the digital age: A critical review and meta-analysis of cyberbullying research among youth. Psychological Bulletin, 140(4), 1073-1137.

96. Lamb, M. E. (2004). *The Role of the Father in Child Development*. Wiley.

97. Lamb, M. E. (2010). The role of the father in child development. New York: Wiley.

98. Lamb, M.E. (2012). The Role of the Father in Child Development. Hoboken, NJ: Wiley.

99. LeBlanc, M. D. (2017). Pediatric anxiety disorders. JAMA Pediatrics, 171(11), 1020-1021.

100. Lerner, R. M., Fisher, C. B., & Weinberg, R. A. (2000). Applying the concept of developmentally appropriate practice to school-age children and youth. Theory Into Practice, 39(4), 277-282.

101. Lim, S. L., & Lim, B. K. (2003). Parenting style and child outcomes in Chinese and immigrant Chinese families-current findings and cross-cultural considerations in conceptualization and research. Marriage & Family Review, 35(3-4), 21-43.

102. Livingstone, S. M. (2016). The class: Living and learning in the digital age. NYU Press.

103. Livingstone, S., & Helsper, E. J. (2007). Taking risks when communicating on the Internet: The role of offline social-psychological factors in young people's vulnerability to online risks. European Journal of Communication, 22(3), 313-325.

104. Maccoby, E. E., & Martin, J. A. (1983). Socialization in the context of the family: Parent-child interaction. In P. H.

Mussen (Ed.), *Handbook of child psychology* (pp. 1-101). New York: Wiley.

105. Maccoby, E. E., & Martin, J. A. (1983). Socialization in the context of the family: Parent-child interaction. In P. H. Mussen (Ed.), Handbook of Child Psychology (4th ed., Vol. 4, pp. 1-101). New York: Wiley.

106. Mandara, J. (2006). The impact of family functioning on African American males' academic achievement: A review and clarification of the empirical literature. Teachers College Record, 108(2), 206-223.

107. Mandara, J., & Murray, C.B. (2002). The effects of parental involvement on academic achievement and mental health of African American males. American Journal of Orthopsychiatry, 72(3), 331-341.

108. Masten, A. S. (2001). Ordinary magic: Resilience processes in development. American Psychologist, 56(3), 227-238.

109. National Institute of Mental Health. (2019). Mental Health Information. Retrieved from https://www.nimh.nih.gov/health

110. National Science Board. (2018). *Science & Engineering Indicators 2018: Women, Minorities, and Persons with Disabilities in Science and Engineering*. National Science Foundation.

111. Nguyen, M. N., & Ryan, A. M. (2008). Does stereotype threat affect test performance of minorities and women? A meta-analysis of experimental evidence. Journal of Applied Psychology, 93(6), 1314-1334.

112. Pleck, J. H. (2012). "Integrating Father Involvement in Parenting Research." Parent Science Practice.

113. Pleck, J. H., & Masciadrelli, B. P. (2004). Paternal Involvement by U.S. Residential Fathers: Levels, Sources, and Consequences. In M. E. Lamb (Ed.), The Role of the Father in Child Development (4th ed., pp. 222-271). Hoboken, NJ: Wiley.

114. Pomerantz, E. M., Ng, F. F., & Wang, Q. (2011). Mothers' affect in the homework context: The importance of staying positive. Developmental Psychology, 47(4), 999-1009.

115. Radesky, J. S., Schumacher, J., & Zuckerman, B. (2016). Mobile and interactive media use by young children: The good, the bad, and the unknown. *Pediatrics, 135*(1), 1-3.

116. Radesky, J. S., Schumacher, J., & Zuckerman, B. (2020). Mobile and Interactive Media Use by Young Children: The Good, the Bad, and the Unknown. Pediatrics, 135(1), 1-3.

117. Rideout, V. J., Foehr, U. G., & Roberts, D. F. (2010). Generation M2: Media in the Lives of 8-to 18-Year-Olds. Henry J. Kaiser Family Foundation.

118. Rideout, V., & Robb, M. B. (2020). The Common Sense Census: Media use by tweens and teens. Common Sense Media.

119. Rinaldi, C. M., & Howe, N. (2012). Mothers' and fathers' parenting styles and associations with toddlers' externalizing, internalizing, and adaptive behaviors. *Early Childhood Research Quarterly*, 27(2), 266-273.

120. Salovey, P., & Mayer, J. D. (1990). Emotional intelligence. *Imagination, Cognition and Personality*, 9(3), 185-211.

121. Shaywitz, S. E., & Shaywitz, B. A. (2008). *Paying attention to reading: The neurobiology of reading and dyslexia*. Development and Psychopathology, 20(4), 1329-1349.

122. Shonkoff, J. P., & Phillips, D. A. (Eds.). (2000). *From Neurons to Neighborhoods: The Science of Early Childhood Development*. National Academies Press.

123. Siegel, D. J., & Bryson, T. P. (2012). The Whole-Brain Child. Bantam Books.

124. Siegel, D. J., & Bryson, T. P. (2012). The Whole-Brain Child. Bantam Books.

125. Siegel, D. J., & Hartzell, M. (2003). Parenting from the Inside Out. New York, NY: Jeremy P. Tarcher/Putnam.

126. Simons, R. L., Whitbeck, L. B., Conger, R. D., & Melby, J. N. (1993). The Effect of Social Support and Parenting Practices on Children's Social Adjustment. Journal of Marriage and Family, 55(2), 356-374.

127. Smith, J., & Jones, A. (2020). "Early Signs of Mental Health Issues in Children." Journal of Child Psychology and Psychiatry, 61(5), 123-135.

128. Smith, R., & Brown, A. (2020). Navigating the Early Childhood Special Needs Landscape. Journal of Special Education Leadership, 33(1), 12-23.

129. Smith, R., Jones, T., & Brown, K. (2015). *Communication strategies for children with autism: a review of current research*. Journal of Autism and Developmental Disorders, 45(10), 35-45.

130. Steinberg, L. (2001). We know some things: Adolescent-parent relationships in retrospect and prospect. Journal of Research on Adolescence, 11(1), 1-19.

131. Steinberg, L. (2001). We know some things: Parent-adolescent relationships in retrospect and prospect. *Journal of Research on Adolescence*, 11(1), 1-19.

132. Steinberg, L. (2001). We know some things: Parent–adolescent relationships in retrospect and prospect. Journal of Research on Adolescence, 11(1), 1-19.

133. Steinberg, L. (2004). The Ten Basic Principles of Good Parenting. Simon & Schuster.

134. Stevenson, H. W., & Stigler, J. W. (1992). <i

135. Sullivan, A. (2013). *Gender Differences in Parenting Styles*. Child Development Journal.

136. Taylor, S. E. (2011). Social support: A review of clinical and experimental approaches. Annual Review of Psychology, 52, 193-214.

137. Taylor, Z. E., Conger, R. D., Robins, R. W., & Widaman, K. F. (2004). Support from Parents, Friends, and Teachers: Adolescent Emotional and Academic Development. Journal of Family Psychology, 18(1), 147-159.

138. Thompson, L., Harris, J., & Fraser, K. (2021). Support Networks for Parents of Children with Disabilities. Family Relations, 70(2), 189-202.

139. Twenge, J. M., Joiner, T. E., Rogers, M. L., & Martin, G. N. (2018). Increases in depressive symptoms, suicide-related outcomes, and suicide rates among U.S adolescents after 2010 and links to increased new media screen time. Clinical Psychological Science, 6(1), 3-17.

140. Valkenburg, P. M., Peter, J., & Schouten, A. P. (2006). Friend networking sites and their relationship to adolescents' well-being and social self-esteem. CyberPsychology & Behavior, 9(5), 584-590.

141. Walker, M. (2017). Why we sleep: Unlocking the power of sleep and dreams. Scribner.

142. White, L., & Brinkerhoff, M. (2011). The impact of early household chores on child development. Journal of Developmental Psychology, 45(3), 712-725.

143. Witt, S. D. (2000). The Influence of Television on Children's Gender Role Socialization. Childhood Education.

144. Wright, B., Leahey, M., & Murphy, F. (2008). The Impact of a Parent-Led Well-Child Clinic on Parenting Practices and Child Development. Journal of Child Health Care, 12(1), 34-48.

www.ingramcontent.com/pod-product-compliance
Lightning Source LLC
Chambersburg PA
CBHW030304100526
44590CB00012B/512